4/10/24

To Our Bridgat
Book Club,

Thank you for all your
support & encouragement
So happy to be a part
of this wonderful group.

Love & best wishes
always

Judi
<3

SUCCESS
REDEFINED

Published by CelebrityPress®, Orlando, FL.

CelebrityPress® is a registered trademark.

Printing and binding at Sheridan

ISBN: 979-8-9892734-0-9
LCCN: 2023919095

Most CelebrityPress® titles are available at special quantity discounts for bulk purchases for sales promotions, premiums, fundraising, and educational use. Special versions or book excerpts can also be created to fit specific needs.

For more information, please write:

CelebrityPress®
3415 W. Lake Mary Blvd. #9550370
Lake Mary, FL 32746
or call 1.877.261.4930

Visit us online at: www.CelebrityPressPublishing.com

SUCCESS
REDEFINED

CelebrityPress®
Lake Mary, Florida

CONTENTS

CHAPTER 1

REDEFINE SUCCESS: DO WHAT YOU LOVE EVERY SINGLE DAY

BY JACK CANFIELD

*None of us can change our yesterdays, but all of us
can change our tomorrows.*
~ Colin Powell
Four-star general and first African-American to become U.S. Secretary of State

Passion. It's what helps über-successful people achieve the extraordinary levels of success they enjoy in their lives. They've determined their life purpose, pursued it with passion, then organized their entire careers, friendships, and lifestyle around it. They've redefined what 'success' means to them. And, in choosing this focused path, they've followed a set of timeless principles that have been used throughout history by other successful people.

When applied, followed and incorporated into your daily life, these principles can bring about the success you are seeking, often creating better results than you ever imagined.

For more than 40 years, my passion has been studying and using these principles to achieve incredible results in my own life. Nearly 20 years ago, I wrote a book called *The Success Principles* to catalog them for aspiring achievers everywhere.

And for four decades, I've been doing what I love...*every single day.*

So what are just a few of these core principles, habits, and behaviors that the world's top achievers use to redefine success for themselves and live the life they want?

FACE WHAT'S NOT WORKING IN
EVERY AREA OF YOUR LIFE

Take an honest look at every major life area. This includes your finances, your relationships, your physical body, your career, and your rest and relaxation time—all of which affect your mindset, your wellbeing and your ability to achieve success. Every one of these high-impact areas has the ability to make or break your future because problems and opportunities in these areas persistently occupy your thoughts.

These areas either add energy or drain energy; they either inspire you or expire you. They help you focus or they take your focus away. They either give you confidence or they make you insecure.

What are these eight high-impact areas that top achievers routinely refine and improve?

Finances	*Health and wellness*
Possessions	*Relationships*
Career	*Personal Growth*
Free time	*Community*

And if you don't like what you see? It's time to make a plan for upgrading, resolving or refining each area to create what you do want.

REDEFINE WHAT SUCCESS
MEANS TO YOU

If you were lucky growing up, you were encouraged to dream big about who you wanted to be when you were older—and what you wanted to have and enjoy during your lifetime. For many of us though, as children our dreams were ignored, or we were told they were silly—or worse, that we would never amount to much. Many of us put aside what we truly wanted in order to get along or avoid conflict. Then as we became adults, we were told to be practical and realistic.

But what about now?

While you may have had to adapt to survive back then, you now know that a bigger, more exciting life is available to you. This is your chance to break free of any negative childhood programming and the adult requirement of 'being practical,' and expand your sense of what's possible, to dream once more, and to envision what you truly want in all the areas of your life.

It's your chance to redefine what 'success' means to you.

1. *Make an 'I Wants' List*

   One of the easiest ways to begin determining what you truly want is to ask a friend to help you make an 'I Wants' list. Have the friend continually ask, "What do you want?" As soon as you answer, have them ask "What do you want?" again. Continue this for about for 10 minutes, while they also jot down their answers. You'll find at first that your 'wants' aren't all that profound. In fact, most people usually hear themselves saying, I want a sports car. I want a house on the beach. But by the end of the 10-minute exercise, the real you begins to speak: *I want people to love me. I want to make a difference. I want to feel powerful*—wants that are true expressions of your core values.

2. *Visualize What You Want*

   While jotting down what you want may be the first time you've ever sat down to dream about your ideal life, there's another—even more powerful—way to succeed in achieving what you want to be, do, and have: visualizing your successful life in the major areas that can literally change *everything* about who you are, what you do, and how you live right now.

   Below are eight major life categories where most of our dreams, goals and achievements live. To truly master the first step toward tremendous success, set aside a few hours to really think about what you want in each category—*and why you want it*. Why is retiring early important to you? Why do you want to live in a million-dollar home? Why do you want to begin studying another language? Will it improve your lifestyle, give you joy, allow you to help others, or something else? Decide what you want to be, do and have—*and why you want that.*

But most importantly, don't hold back when thinking about what you want. Give yourself permission to list anything and everything that comes to mind. Don't edit your dreams because they're too expensive, too difficult, different from anything you've ever done before, or 'not acceptable' to your family and friends. No one else needs to approve what you write—or even see it. This is for YOU. Dream big.

3. *Visualize Your Finances*

Begin this exercise by listening to some relaxing music and sitting quietly in a comfortable environment. Then, start visualizing your ideal life exactly as if you are living it.

First, visualize your financial situation. How much money do you have in your savings? How much income do you make? What is your net worth? How is your cash flow?

4. *Visualize Your Possessions*

Next, visualize what your dream house—your 'forever home'— would look like. What style of house is it? Where is it located? What color is the interior? How is it furnished? Are there paintings on the walls? What do they look like? Walk through your perfect house visually, using your mind's eye.

At this point, don't worry about how you'll get that house. Don't sabotage yourself by saying, *I can't live in Hawaii because I don't make enough money.* Once you give your mind's eye the picture, your mind will solve the 'not enough money' challenge. Simply be honest with yourself about what you truly want. Continue visualizing your perfect home. Does it include extensive property, gardens, stables, unique views, a guesthouse, an art studio or other unique characteristics?

Next, visualize what kind of car you are driving, followed by other possessions you might acquire. Do you own a boat? Where is it harbored? Do you have valuable artwork, an extensive library, designer or antique furnishings, important art objects or unique collectibles?

5. *Visualize Your Work, Career or Business*

Next, visualize what you are doing in your career. Where are you working? Who are you working with? What is your compensation like? Is it your own business? What kind of clients do you have?

Have you pursued higher education and earned a degree? Are you in management, outreach, advocacy, or some other unique role?

6. *Visualize Your Relationships*

Move on to visualizing the perfect relationships you want in your life. What is the quality of your relationships with your family? Who are your friends? What do those friendships feel like? Are they loving, supportive, and empowering? Could they be better? How are your needs getting met in your relationships?

7. *Visualize Your Free Time*

Next, focus on your rest, relaxation and recreation time. What are you doing with your family and friends in the free time you've created for yourself? What hobbies are you pursuing? What kinds of vacations do you take? Are you traveling to exotic locales? Are you spending a month or two in a specific place?

8. *Visualize Your Health and Fitness*

Then, visualize your ideal body, your physical health, and your emotional state. Are you free and open, relaxed, and in an ecstatic state of bliss all day long? What does that look and feel like?

What are you doing to stay fit and healthy? What kinds of foods are you eating and how are they prepared? Are you practicing daily meditation, yoga, tai chi, mindfulness or some other regular practice?

9. *Visualize Your Personal and Spiritual Growth*

What about your own personal growth? Do you see yourself going back to school, taking training, seeking therapy for a past hurt, or otherwise growing in confidence? Are you actively pursuing a spiritual life including belonging to a church, pursuing religious education or daily study, traveling to sacred places, or volunteering for mission work?

10. *Visualize Making a Difference and Being of Service*

Finally, think about the 'community' you've chosen to live in. It might be a geographic location or a community of like-minded people scattered around the world. What does it look like? What kinds of activities take place?

Think about being of service to others. What charitable work are you pursuing? What are you doing to make a difference? How often do you participate in these activities? Who are you helping? How are their lives being changed?

11. *Share Your Vision for Maximum Impact*

Finally, when you've created a vivid picture in your mind and written down the details of the life you want, share your vision with somebody. This can be very uncomfortable. In fact, most people believe, I can't share that! It's too personal. *What I want is crazy. People will think I'm weird.* But the truth is that half the people you talk to will want many of the same things.

Everyone wants material wealth, loving relationships, supportive family and friends, and time to help make a difference in our world. But too few of us readily admit it. Sharing your vision helps your subconscious mind become accountable to making it happen.

SET GOALS TO ACHIEVE YOUR NEW DEFINITION OF SUCCESS

Once you decide what you want in each of the eight areas above, you can begin to break down your lifestyle 'wants' into small, achievable goals that will eventually bring about the life you want.

In fact, extensive study has shown that—once we decide what we want and set a goal around it—the brain actually helps us bring about these life-changing results. For instance, experts know that when you give it a goal, the brain triggers its *reticular activating system*—a web of neuro-pathways that filters through the millions of random images, facts and information we're bombarded with each day—then sends to our conscious mind those bits of data that will help us achieve our goals. When you give the brain an image of something you want to achieve, it will labor around the clock to find ways to achieve the picture you put there. Without a doubt, the brain is a goal-seeking instrument.

> *Goals are dreams with deadlines.*
> ~ Diana Scharf Hunt
> Author of The Tao of Time

12. *How Much By When?*

Considering that your brain is working for you, it makes sense to be *specific* about your goals. When I teach about goal-setting, I stress the importance of setting goals that are both *measurable* and *time-specific*.

Measurable—The most powerful goals are those that are measurable, both by you and by others. For instance, your goal might be to generate a specific number of new clients for your new consulting firm so you can meet your income goals. By knowing the required number, you can focus on marketing campaigns, referral agreements and other systems that will hit that number.

Time-specific—Your goal should also be *time-specific*. In other words, not only should you state *how much* you'll earn, but also *by when* you'll earn it. Only with both these units of measure can you determine whether you've achieved your goal. You also become accountable to meeting your deadline.

Additionally, by being so specific, you can focus on the emotions you'll be feeling when you achieve your goal. Your brain knows the payoff from hitting the target.

When you decide on the model of car you'll buy with your new-found income, the kind of house you'll live in, or which private schools your children will attend, you can't help but feel the positive emotions attached to those images. When you add emotion, color, detail, and features to visualizing your goals, your brain will begin in earnest to seek out ways to fulfill them.

13. *A Breakthrough Goal Can Amplify Your Entire Life*

Perhaps the true benefit of any goal is that—by pursuing it—you become a more confident, capable person. No one can ever take away the person you become as a result of pursuing your loftiest goals.

In addition to your many weekly and monthly goals, I recommend that you create *one single goal* such that, in the process of achieving it, you upgrade every aspect of your life—from your finances to your friends, your business success, your lifestyle and more. Wouldn't that be a goal you would want to work on constantly and pursue with enthusiasm?

I call that a Breakthrough Goal.

For instance, if you were a consultant and you knew that you could land big tech companies as clients by speaking at the annual industry conference, wouldn't you work night and day to achieve that goal?

And if you partnered with smaller consulting firms to provide specific services that you can't do yourself, wouldn't that grow your business, your income, and your status in the industry—leading to other opportunities and a far more important network of connections than you have right now?

It would uplevel everything you do in your career and amplify who you are as a person. That's an example of a Breakthrough Goal.

TAKE ACTION TO ACHIEVE YOUR NEW DEFINITION OF SUCCESS

In the world today, most people are rewarded for action, not for ideas. Yet it's surprising how many people get caught up in planning, investigating and other preliminary activity when what they really should be doing is *taking action* on their goals.

When you take action, the Universe rewards that action with additional help that can speed you on your way. You also gain feedback about your chosen path or methods.

> *Things may come to those who wait,*
> *but only the things left by those who hustle.*
> ~ Abraham Lincoln
> 16th President of the United States

14. *The World Pays for What You Do, Not for What You Know*

Many people have had good ideas—some of which led to entirely new industries or never-before-seen ways of making money. The Internet in its infancy was a place where many people had good ideas. But how many of those people took action and created the Google's, Amazon's, Facebook's and other businesses we know today?

The fact is that, while most people know *a lot* about making money or getting results or creating advancement in the world, only a few actually get to *enjoy the rewards* of this knowledge (whether financial, professional or otherwise) simply because the rest don't take action on their ideas.

Successful people, on the other hand, have a bias for action.

More than any other characteristic, action is what separates the successful from the unsuccessful—the people who actually reap the rewards from those who would merely like to.

Perhaps you, too, had a great idea at one time—only to see it turned into a successful business or a new invention or a popular product *by someone else* because they took action and you did not.

The reality is that, in the world today, the people who are rewarded are those who take action. We're paid for what we do.

*   *   *   *   *

21

THESE PRINCIPLES WORK, IF YOU WORK THE PRINCIPLES

In the end, the results you enjoy in your life are a product of your habits, behaviors, thoughts and actions. When you redefine what success means to you, when you become specific about the results you want—then set goals, take action, and focus on achieving them—your life will transform. You'll bring about the success and results you want.

By consistently acting upon these success principles, the only limiting factor will be your imagination and ability to dream about your future.

About Jack

Known as America's #1 Success Coach, Jack Canfield is the Founder and Chairman of the Canfield Training Group in Santa Barbara, California, which trains and coaches entrepreneurs, corporate leaders, managers, sales professionals, educators, and the general public in how to accelerate the achievement of their personal, professional and financial goals.

Jack Canfield is best known as the co-author of the #1 New York Times bestselling *Chicken Soup for the Soul®* book series, which has sold more than 600 million books in 49 languages, including 41 New York Times bestsellers.

As the CEO of Chicken Soup for the Soul Enterprises, he helped grow the *Chicken Soup for the Soul®* brand into a virtual empire of books, children's books, audios, videos, CDs, classroom materials, a syndicated column, and a television show, as well as a vigorous program of licensed products that includes everything from clothing and board games to nutraceuticals and a successful line of Chicken Soup for the Pet Lover's Soul® cat and dog foods.

His other books include *The Success Principles™: How to Get from Where You Are to Where You Want to Be* (now available in its 10th Anniversary Edition), *The Success Principles Workbook, The Success Principles for Teens, The Aladdin Factor, Dare to Win, Heart at Work, The Power of Focus: How to Hit Your Personal, Financial and Business Goals with Absolute Certainty, You've Got to Read This Book, Tapping into Ultimate Success, Jack Canfield's Key to Living the Law of Attraction, The 30-Day Sobriety Solution* and his recent autobiographical novel, *The Golden Motorcycle Gang: A Story of Transformation*.

Jack is a dynamic speaker and was inducted into the National Speakers Association's Speakers Hall of Fame. He has appeared on more than 1,000 radio and television shows, including *Oprah, Montel, Larry King Live, The Today Show, Fox and Friends,* and two different hour-long PBS Specials devoted exclusively to his work. Jack is also a featured teacher in 12 movies, including *The Secret, The Meta-Secret, The Truth, The Keeper of the Keys, Tapping into the Source,* and *The Tapping Solution.* Jack was also honored with a documentary produced about his life and teachings called, *The Soul of Success: The Jack Canfield Story.*

Jack has personally helped hundreds of thousands of people on six continents become multi-millionaires, business leaders, best-selling authors, leading sales professionals, successful entrepreneurs, and world-class athletes while at the same time creating balanced, fulfilling, and healthy lives.

His corporate clients have included Virgin Records, SONY Pictures, Daimler-Chrysler, Federal Express, GE, Johnson & Johnson, Microsoft, Merrill Lynch, Campbell's Soup, Re/Max, The Million Dollar Forum, The Million Dollar Roundtable, The Young Entrepreneurs Organization, The Young Presidents Organization, the Executive Committee, and the World Business Council. He is the founder of the Transformational Leadership Council and a member of Evolutionary Leaders, two groups devoted to helping create a world that works for everyone.

Jack is a graduate of Harvard, earned his M.Ed. from the University of Massachusetts, and has received three honorary doctorates in psychology and public service. He is married, has three children, two step-children, and two grandsons.

For more information, visit:

• www.JackCanfield.com.

CHAPTER 2

THE PARADOX OF SUCCESS: HIDDEN STRUGGLES OF HIGH-PERFORMING PROFESSIONALS

BY NANCY HO

SUCCESS

It seems like such a simple word to describe and define, doesn't it?

To most people, 'success' is synonymous with the status that's achieved when one appears to have made it to the peak of their profession.

While these situations often bring a sense of accomplishment and achievement, they don't always equate to finally finding fulfilment for the person who's just dedicated decades to climbing those steps to success, do they?

After all, we still hear heart-wrenching stories of 'successful people' who seemingly have it all (the fortune and the fame). Yet, despite appearing to have it all, these same people end up in despair and depression.

From the outside, other people may ponder – "What could they possibly be lacking in their life?" From the inside, this person may still be silently searching for meaning beyond surface-level success. These two polar opposite perspectives set the stage for this professional paradox.

You see, these professionals feel like they've sacrificed so much for society's definition of success. But when they finally face the facts, they still feel empty and exhausted at the end of their day.

If this feels familiar to you, then please keep reading. Because after studying High Performance Professionals (HPP's) for decades, I've pulled together a framework – backed by science, surveys, and statistics – for you to follow, so that you finally find fulfilment by shrinking the gap between success and satisfaction.

But before we delve deeper and explore the implications of leaving this emptiness unchecked, I wanted you to know how personal this professional paradox is to me, so you realize that I can relate to and resonate with you.

DO PRIVILEGE, PRESTIGE, AND PROSPERITY ALWAYS PAVE THE PATH TO PERSONAL PEACE?

Born into a prosperous Southeast Asian family in the 60s, some could consider my life a life of privilege. Elite schools in Singapore, real estate in prime locations, higher education spanning Switzerland and the UK ¬– by any measure, I had a head start.

My race towards success was largely shaped by my late father, a guiding star whose influence touched my life even before I was born. His time with me was brief, just the first three years of my life, but his belief in my uniqueness and potential continues to echo within me even to this day. Supported by my loving family, I chose to internalize his vision of me earning a significant income, achieving significant influence, and subsequently being placed in a position to make a significant impact in the world – and it became my 'North Star'.

Yet, despite tasting society's definition of success due to my own entrepreneurial efforts (even as early as age 13), I still grappled with an unsettling emptiness.

Material wealth and the status that came with it were my initial yardsticks that I used to measure success. I felt like I'd already won this race early on in my life, becoming a financially free High-Performing Professional by 25 years old. However, shortly thereafter, I felt like I'd raced so hard only to stumble near what I thought was the finish line. Because, a healthcare scare at the age of 28 forced me to confront a vast inner void, and this wake-up call resulted in a radical revaluation within me of what success really meant – on my own terms.

Can you begin to paint a picture in your own mind of the weight that societal expectations have placed on you, and how those expectations may have steered you away from your truest forms of fulfilment?

THE PROFESSIONAL PARADOX
MOST PEOPLE MISS

Success, as traditionally defined, is a paradox. On one hand, it is often equated with tangible achievements such as wealth, status, and power. High Performing Professionals (HPPs) are typically seen as the epitome of success, having climbed the corporate ladder, amassed significant wealth, and earned the respect and admiration of their peers. Yet, on the other hand, these external markers of success often fail to bring the happiness and satisfaction they promise.

This paradox arises from the dichotomy between external achievements and internal fulfilment. External achievements are visible, quantifiable, and often subject to societal validation. They're the milestones that society encourages us to strive for, the benchmarks by which we compare ourselves to others. However, these achievements, while significant, aren't always synonymous with satisfaction – and subsequently happiness.

Internal fulfilment, on the other hand, is deeply personal and subjective. It's about feeling content, at peace, and satisfied with who we are and the life we lead. It's about living in alignment with our values, passions, and purpose. Unlike external achievements, internal fulfilment cannot be measured or validated by others. It's a deeply personal journey that varies from one individual to another.

The paradox of success lies in the fact that while HPPs often excel in achieving external markers of success, they can still feel a void within. They may have everything society deems necessary for a successful life, yet still feel unfulfilled and dissatisfied.

This professional paradox challenges the conventional definition of success and prompts us to reconsider what true success really means. It suggests that true success is not just about achieving external markers, but also about finding internal fulfilment and personal satisfaction.

THE HIDDEN STRUGGLES OF HIGH-PERFORMING PROFESSIONALS

High-Performing Professionals (HPPs) are often seen as the epitome of success. They've climbed the corporate ladder, amassed significant wealth, and earned the respect and admiration of their peers. Yet, beneath this veneer of success lie hidden struggles that are rarely discussed or acknowledged.

One of the most significant challenges faced by HPPs is the immense pressure to perform. This pressure can come from various sources - the expectations of superiors, the demands of clients, the competition with peers, and often, their own high standards. The need to constantly perform at peak levels can lead to chronic stress, which can have serious implications for both mental and physical health.

The stress of high performance can manifest in various ways. Mentally, it can lead to anxiety, depression, and burnout. High-Performing Professionals may find themselves constantly worrying about their performance, feeling overwhelmed by their responsibilities, or losing motivation and passion for their work. Physically, chronic stress can lead to a host of health issues, including insomnia, heart disease, and weakened immune system.

Another hidden struggle of HPPs is the lack of work-life balance. The demands of their careers often leave little time for personal pursuits or relationships. They may find themselves missing out on important family events, neglecting their hobbies, or feeling disconnected from their friends and loved ones. This imbalance can lead to feelings of isolation and loneliness, further exacerbating the stress and dissatisfaction they feel.

Moreover, High-Performing Professionals often struggle with the paradox of success. Despite their external achievements, they may feel a void within, a sense of unfulfillment that can't be filled by professional success alone. They may question the purpose and meaning of their work, feeling as though they are stuck in a cycle of achieving for the sake of achieving, without deriving any real satisfaction or joy.

These hidden struggles of HPPs are rarely discussed, yet they are real and significant. They highlight the need for a different definition of success, one that encompasses not just professional achievements, but also personal fulfilment, well-being, and meaningful relationships. By acknowledging and addressing these struggles, HPPs can begin to navigate their way towards a more balanced and fulfilling life.

REDEFINING SUCCESS: A MORE APPROPRIATE APPROACH IN TOUCH WITH THE TIMES

In the fast-paced, achievement-oriented world we inhabit, it's all too easy to equate success with professional accomplishments and financial prosperity. This conventional success model often leaves High-Performing Professionals (HPPs) feeling short of fulfilment and satisfaction. It's time we shake up this outdated viewpoint and re-envision what true success encompasses.

The truth is, success isn't a monolithic concept. It's an intensely personal and varied journey, differing greatly from one person to another. For some, it could revolve around professional accolades or a particular income bracket. Yet for others, it might pivot on making a tangible difference in their community or leading a balanced life. The power to define success lies uniquely within your grasp.

Expanding our definition of success, it should encapsulate more than just career advancements and monetary gains. It should include personal fulfilment, well-being, and the creation of meaningful relationships. It's about crafting a life that resonates with your core values, passions, and purpose.

Personal fulfilment becomes a cornerstone in this reimagined definition of success. It focuses on pursuing what truly sparks joy within you, rather than simply following societal norms. It's about setting and achieving goals that align with your core values, infusing your life with a sense of joy and satisfaction. Remember, personal fulfilment is not a final destination, but a continuous journey of growth and self-discovery.

Physical and mental well-being form the bedrock of success. In their quest for professional accomplishments, HPPs may often overlook their health. Yet, without good health, the joys of success are diminished. Prioritizing self-care, maintaining a balanced lifestyle, and seeking support when necessary, are not just luxuries but necessities.

Mental well-being, particularly, is a silent pillar of success, often neglected but as critical as physical health. Stress, anxiety, and burnout should not be viewed as badges of honour, but signals indicating the need for change.

Finally, the role of meaningful relationships in defining success can't be overstated. We are inherently social creatures, and our connections with others fuel our sense of success. Whether they are professional relationships, friendships, or family ties, these bonds provide support during trying times and amplify our happiness in times of joy. They enhance our life's quality, contributing significantly to our overall fulfilment.

In redefining success, we aren't dismissing the importance of professional achievements or material wealth. Instead, we're suggesting they should not stand as the only markers of success. By widening our success scope to embrace personal fulfilment, well-being, and meaningful relationships, we can stride toward more balanced, rewarding, and authentically successful lives.

So, are you ready to redefine success on your terms?

FOCUSING ON FULFILMENT: A REAL-WORLD ROADMAP FOR HIGH-PERFORMING PROFESSIONALS

Your voyage towards fulfilment is not linear; rather, it's a winding road, ripe with opportunities for self-exploration, growth, and transformation. For High-Performing Professionals (HPPs), this expedition often demands a profound reassessment of their success benchmarks and significant life adjustments.

The following simple strategies can serve as signposts, guiding HPPs towards finally finding the fulfilment they deeply desire and believe they deserve.

1 - Introspection:

The fundamental first step towards leading a life of feeling fulfilled is introspection. This requires a temporary retreat from life's current chaos to reflect profoundly on what matters most to you. A simple starting point would be to begin to ask yourself the following questions:

- *What values and virtues do you possess that can act as your new 'North Star'?*

- *What instils a sense of joy and satisfaction within you regardless of how much money you make?*

- *Which aspects of your life breed stress or discontent?*

Genuine introspection can illuminate the necessary adjustments needed to harmonize your life with your authentic self. Though it may not always provide comfort, it indisputably serves as a pivotal step towards achieving personal contentment.

2 - Individual Improvement:

Fulfilment is closely tied to personal growth. It's about continuously learning, evolving, and pushing your boundaries. This could involve pursuing a new hobby, learning a new skill, or seeking personal development opportunities. It could also mean addressing personal weaknesses or seeking therapy to overcome mental health challenges.

Personal growth contributes to a sense of accomplishment and self-efficacy, which are key components of fulfilment.

3 - Integrating Your Personal and Professional Life:

For many HPPs, the line between work and personal life often blurs, leading to burnout and dissatisfaction. Achieving work-life balance is not about equally dividing time between work and personal life, but rather about finding a balance that works for you.

This could involve setting boundaries, delegating tasks, or making time for relaxation and leisure activities. It's about creating a lifestyle that allows you to excel in your professional life while also enjoying personal time and maintaining your health.

4 - Interpersonal Investment:

Relationships play a crucial role in our sense of fulfilment. They provide support, love, and a sense of belonging. For HPPs, it's important to invest time and effort in cultivating meaningful relationships. This could involve spending quality time with family and friends, strengthening connections with colleagues, or seeking new social opportunities. It's also about being present in these interactions and genuinely valuing these relationships.

5 - Investing Intrinsically:

Lastly, self-care is an essential part of the path to fulfilment. It's about prioritizing your physical and mental health. This could involve regular exercise, a healthy diet, adequate sleep, practicing mindfulness, meditation or other stress management techniques. Self-care is not a luxury but a necessity for overall well-being and fulfilment.

The path to fulfilment is a personal journey that requires commitment, effort, and patience. However, by embracing self-reflection, personal growth, work-life balance, meaningful relationships, and self-care, HPPs can find greater fulfilment and satisfaction in their lives.

FINDING FULFILMENT IS THE ONLY METRIC THAT MATTERS

Please allow me to paint a picture so that we can put things into perspective. In this picture, you're a High-Performing Professional (HPP) standing at the peak of your professional prowess – and you've got the prestige, power, and prosperity to prove it.

On paper, you're a symbol of success. Yet deep within, emptiness expands. You stand alone in the shining spotlight of your own success, the cruel irony of the situation not lost on you - *the more you've gained, the less fulfilled you feel.* It's a puzzling paradox that often appears for professionals like you and me.

Yes, this was once my story as well. I treaded this treacherous tightrope too, burdened by the weight of other people's expectations and relentless demand to perform. I've felt the brunt of this battle that was waged against me daily and learned the bitter truth – *the traditional tools we use to measure success often fail to measure the satisfaction we seek.*

Left untended, this unhappiness and unfulfillment threatens to consume all aspects of your life. It's a journey through a seemingly endless night, a path I urge you not to walk alone.

Changing the narrative requires redefining the very concept of success. A fulfilling life embraces professional achievements and material wealth but also places equal emphasis on what matters most. It prompts you to adjust your compass from societal norms to your deepest intrinsic desires.

In my own tale, I walked through the dark tunnel of unfulfillment, emerged into the light and discovered a new definition of success. I found a place where professional accomplishments and personal satisfaction live in harmony. Now, my life is a balanced blend of professional prosperity, personal joy, and authentic contentment.

As I close this chapter of our shared narrative, I extend a friendly invitation. Let me be your guide as we rewrite your future together, *transitioning from a life that appears successful to one that feels deeply satisfying.*

Leading with Love,
Nancy Ho

About Nancy

Nancy Ho is an internationally-recognized Executive Coach renowned for her ground breaking approach towards assisting high-performing professionals (HPPs) in bridging the gap between professional success and personal satisfaction. With over 26 years of experience as a Life and Business Strategist and Transformative Coach, Nancy is skilled at guiding you towards an integrated and harmonious personal and professional life.

With a name etched in major magazines such as *Expat Living, Ezhealth, Mothership,* and *Conscious Living,* Nancy's impact reverberates through the industry. Her book, *Love Reignited,* stands as a testament to her distinctive ability to resolve conflicts and strengthen relationships. She's also shared the international stage with luminaries like Dr. Phil, Deepak Chopra, JT Foxx, Moira Forbes, Hugh Hilton, Adam Coffey and George Ross, reinforcing her influence and credibility.

Nancy's career is rooted in her personal journey. Having wrestled with pain, depression, and a serious health scare, she has triumphed over adversity to achieve success. Today, she stands as a beacon of hope for those battling similar challenges. Her ethos is not about success measured by wealth or status, but the fulfilment derived from living a life of choice and desire.

She understands the unique challenges faced by HPPs. Lack of fulfilment despite professional success, the struggle to balance work with personal life, stagnation in mindset, relationship conflicts, residual stress, and unresolved past trauma are all too common in their lives. She addresses these problems by unearthing their root causes and providing a fresh understanding of life's intricacies.

Today, Nancy continues her mission, dedicated to guiding high achievers like you to a life of fulfilment, success, and equanimity. Partner with Nancy Ho, and allow her to illuminate your path to a future of greater success and personal satisfaction. Let her guide you towards a life lived by design, not by default.

Nancy dismisses ineffective methods like positive thinking or superficial interventions. Instead, she focuses on developing clarity, defining purpose, and crafting a vision for a promising future. Her expertise extends to tackling Imposter Syndrome, managing pandemic-induced fatigue, and resolving psychosomatic illnesses, ultimately leading to a boost in personal performance and inner well-being.

Nancy's clientele is not limited to anyone. Whether it's a CEO trying to maximize their team's potential, an entrepreneur seeking personal fulfilment, or a top sales professional aspiring for an action-oriented mindset, she offers tailored solutions for all. This transformative journey, however, is only for those ready to take back control of their lives, break free from the constraints of their past, and design a life of confidence, positivity, and assurance.

In a world where time is limited, Nancy's philosophy is about maximizing one's potential, living authentically, and leaving behind a legacy. Her enduring message resonates with those who have reached the zenith of professional success but yearn for personal satisfaction. Let her guide you towards a life lived by design, not by default.

To learn more about or contact Nancy, visit:

- www.nancyho.net
- https://www.facebook.com/Happynancy03
- https://www.linkedin.com/in/nancy-ho-46370567/
- nancy@nancyho.net

CHAPTER 3

FROM CORPORATE TO CALLING—EMBRACING A PURPOSEFUL LIFE

BY ANA MEGRELISHVILI

I have restarted my career, and to some degree my life, twice.

RIDING HIGH IN GEORGIA

I was living in Georgia, a small country in Eastern Europe, a country sandwiched between the ancient empires of Turkey and Russia. I was 19 and second in command of the largest nonprofit in the country, bringing in a yearly salary higher than most in my country could dream of. There wasn't a week that I wasn't on television or meeting with a politician, ambassador, or someone else with an important title. For a nineteen-year-old, it was easy to feel like I was riding high.

However, that high became a fall when the bottom dropped out – the promotion I'd need to take full charge of the nonprofit as the director was taken away because I did not have a university degree, particularly from a big-name foreign university.

That moment, once the fog cleared, was when I decided to start over.

I needed to move to the United States, get my degree in International Studies, and then return to Georgia – I'd prove to everyone else and myself that I could do it.

ARRIVING IN THE USA

In 2008, I got accepted into Berea College, a small liberal arts college in Kentucky, and relocated to the United States as a full-time student with a suitcase full of dreams.

So here I was, slowing down to accelerate. I gave up my successful career to become a first-year student yet again. It was difficult to accept my new reality initially, but I knew I had to; I was forced to return to the success I knew, to grow again.

The acquisition of wealth was my primary motivator for a while. It's what all the movies said to do. I was pursuing my promotions, raises, fashion, and fancy vacations for about ten years until a dissatisfaction with this American dream started growing within. I felt that there had to be more to life than constantly working 12-hour days, living to have a vacation once or twice a year, and being a consumer. The desire to have a positive impact on this world would keep me up at night as I tried to figure out my purpose on this Earth we call home.

I hired a career coach to help me organize my thoughts, knowing I wouldn't do the job myself. I didn't know where to turn.

LIFE WITH A COACH

I was in the top 1%; how could I be unhappy?

Through my coaching sessions, I gained clarity that no amount of money would be able to satisfy my yearning to live a purposeful life. The problem was that I did not know what that meant for me. I knew I had to figure it out and find my authentic self.

In 2022, I quit my corporate career and took a year sabbatical to find my purpose in life. Again, it felt like I was pushing the brakes on my personal growth and downgrading myself from a successful career.

However, putting on the brakes is where the change came. Within a year of my sabbatical, I found my authentic self and true passion, discovering that rare gem that was buried deep inside me the entire time.

Within twelve months, I traveled to twelve countries, wrote three books, and started two new businesses. In my personal life, I reconciled with my mother, surrounded myself with like-minded friends who love and support me, and found a loving, romantic relationship that brought me joy for the first time in my life.

THE BIRTH OF CHRISTIAN PROFESSIONALS OF ATLANTA

"Why is it so hard to meet other Christians?"

"I don't know, but you're right."

A best friend and I were sitting at a table, aggravated at our lack of connection in the community we were part of – Metro Atlanta.

"We've been here for so long, but it feels like we don't know anybody."

A simple Google search right there at the table for 'Christian meetups' or 'Christian professional organizations in Atlanta' led to zero results.

"Why not do it ourselves?"

I could feel the fire in my spirit stoking up at the idea. It was time to go back to my roots whether I knew it consciously or not. We instantly started to think of the mission statement: *Our mission is to bring together Christian professionals in Atlanta to develop meaningful relationships through common faith, values, and philanthropy.*

Christian Professionals of Atlanta took off quickly. Today, Christian Professionals of Atlanta continues to grow, bringing business leaders within Atlanta together, and encouraging them to become stronger servant leaders. Each month a nonprofit is invited to share their mission with the group to drum up interest and have members participate in activities they hold close to their hearts. We participate in service projects to benefit the Atlanta area multiple times yearly.

An incredible thing happens when you play into a mission that serves your community. People want to become part of something bigger than themselves. They want to join a movement that brings positive change. You'll find yourself surrounded by those who want to make a change.

Within a short period, Christian Professionals of Atlanta became a brand, with many prominent professionals joining as members. I envision having a map of the United States hanging in my office with pins in every single state, noting the existence of the chapter of my organization. That's what it is all about, having the bold vision to propel the needle forward.

A NEW BEGINNING – COACHING AND LEARNING

I started my coaching business, Find Courage to Change, while I was already busy building Christian Professionals of Atlanta. While I wasn't looking to start another business, it found me. Something in my spirit demanded that I give the idea the attention it deserves.

During the development time it took to grow Find Courage to Change, a book, *Finding Courage to Change*, was born. In fact, writing the book was my healing journey finding a way to make its way to the light of day. *Finding Courage to Change* explores overcoming childhood trauma and not letting it define who you are as an adult. In fact, I donate 25% of the book's sales to Saprea, an organization that exists to liberate our society from child sexual abuse, and I am passionate about supporting their cause.

The more I started talking about the topic of my book with clients and new connections, the more I was answering questions, having professionals seek my guidance, and people share very personal details about their lives. I knew I had to figure out a way to help them. There was no way I could just let them down.

Knowing another calling was knocking, I pursued Personal Excellence Life Coach certification. I began my business to start coaching people and help them become better versions of themselves. I help my clients figure out what they truly want and how to get there – from A-Z. I focus on breaking limiting beliefs, giving clients the tools to shift their mindset to be full, expansive, and abundant. As humans, we become our own prison keepers. I guide toward unlocking the box humans put themselves in, and liberating them into the vibrant world that is full of potential.

TRADITIONS AND UPBRINGING

Our traditions and upbringing can make us feel judged by our community if we don't follow established paths or focus on practicality.

However, I could embrace my creativity, passions, and purpose by breaking down my conventional lifestyle. This led to a life beyond my expectations. I learned to live in the moment and not conform to societal expectations. I allowed myself to dream, envision, and imagine what happiness and purpose mean. I treated my past experiences as a sacred gift and shared them with others.

My purpose in this book is to pass on the message that change is good for evolution, healing, and growth. I encourage others to be agents of change, pushing people outside their comfort zones and walking on this exciting journey called life.

I also encourage you to let go of fear and take a leap of faith toward the life you envision for yourself.

WHAT YOU CAN LEARN FROM MY JOURNEY

Many people are afraid of change.

Most only decide to make a change when their comfort zone becomes too uncomfortable for them, when it isn't a comfort zone anymore. However, those occasions are relatively rare in the scope of a person's complete life, meaning there aren't many opportunities to be forced to learn.

...Ask yourself the three big questions:

1. What am I doing to change the situation that I am unhappy about?
2. What's the possible worst-case scenario if I make this change?
3. What will I gain if I make this change?

Question 1: *"What am I doing to change the situation that I am unhappy about?"*

When I was unhappy with my corporate career, I realized that I should not complain about it if my answer to the question of: "What am I doing to change the situation that I am unhappy about?" is: "I am doing nothing about it." If I am doing nothing to change the situation I am in, I am wasting my breath complaining about it. Then, I either need to accept the situation or I need to put some action behind making the change. I made the decision to make the change and take a year of sabbatical.

Question Two: *"What will be the worst-case scenario for me?"*

The worst case would have been that I did not find my purpose and, after taking this break, effectively put my 'normal' life on hold. I would have had to return to my corporate career without discovering anything, like an explorer who comes home empty-handed.

I thought, "That's not catastrophic. I would get amazing experiences and a much-needed break out of it. It might cost me, sure, but I can make that money back."

Time is the most valuable asset in life, one that you cannot earn back, save up, or get more of. I was buying my time for that year to explore what I wanted my life to look like, knowing the risk involved.

Question Three: *"What will I gain if I make this change?"*

You can look at this question as the best-case scenario. In my case, it would be finding my purpose and mission, thus the happiness and fulfillment I have sought and yearned for so long. The results I achieved surpassed my best-case scenario expectations tenfold. Everything I am doing now will become my legacy. Something that will exist long after I am gone. Looking back, it was absolutely worth it, taking this leap of faith and living from my savings for a year to achieve the life I've always dreamed of. The result was that coming to this country and receiving an amazing education that allowed me to accelerate my career beyond my imagination. In the United States, I received better pay, much faster advancement in my career, and the ability to acquire wealth that was beyond my imagination, more than I could ever achieve in Georgia.

Let me be honest; while I'm financially earning less than I used to during my corporate career, I have elevated myself to a higher level in society, where I now meet successful business owners, politicians, and famous people on my own accord and at their level. I am pursuing my dreams, which I'm sure will take me way further than my corporate career could ever have taken me. I recognize that my example of change is quite grand. However, these three questions are a great general guide that will work on any area of your life you are unhappy about.

Remember, modern society tells us that success is moving up in the hierarchy of a large corporation, earning a certain amount, living in a certain neighborhood, and driving a certain car. If this is the case, and society is correct, why are so many people so unhappy with their lives and so miserable in their careers?

RECAP

1. Once you identify the area where you want to change, get rid of fear by defining the worst- and best-case scenarios for what this change will bring.
2. Define what success means to you and start working toward your dream life. It could be your romantic relationship, career, friendships, or health; the process is still the same.
3. Write down the answers to the three questions outlined above and put them away so you can look at them again when you need a lift.

This world deserves to see what you are about to accomplish.

About Ana

Ana Megrelishvili is the CEO and co-founder of Christian Professionals of Atlanta, a networking organization focused on bringing Atlanta's leaders together to achieve a positive impact on the community through service.

Ana's passion for making a positive impact on the world has taken her on the path of working with nonprofits when she became a board member of Gift-Wrapping Stars for Children and gala committee chair for Saprea. Ana helps adults find their own path to positive change in their lives through her coaching business, Find Courage to Change.

As a thriving adult of childhood abuse, Ana is making efforts to educate people about her healing journey and spread a message of hope to people she encounters who also went through similar experiences. She documents her journey to healing in her book, *Finding Courage to Change*.

Ana documents her journey of moving to the United States from the Republic of Georgia in Eastern Europe in the book, *Powerful Female Immigrants: Volume 3*.

Ana holds a BS in Business Management from Berea College and an MBA from the University of Kentucky. She enjoys Latin dancing, volunteering, and creating new recipes in her free time.

Learn more at:

- www.findcouragetochange.com
- www.cpofatl.com

CHAPTER 4

MAKE YOUR BUSINESS MISSION-DRIVEN! THE THREE-STAGE PROCESS TO BEAT THE CURVE

BY NICK NANTON

The brand was at a standstill.

Dove Soap, a product created in 1953 by Lever Brothers, had been a steady seller since its inception. Its innovative 'beauty bar,' a soap that was composed of one-quarter cleansing cream, was sold on the basis of straightforward marketing messages touting its uniqueness. Taglines such as 'Dove Won't Dry Your Skin Like Soap Can' and 'Dove is Good for Your Skin' had a built-in appeal to its female target audience, and, by the 1990's, it was a $200 million brand.

By the early 2000's, however, Dove had seemingly flown as high as it could with its traditional marketing approach. Up until then, the beauty brand, like its competition, had always used attractive models to demonstrate its product – but more and more, those attractive models seemed like an alien species to the majority of women. Result? Dove seemed like a dated commodity that was quickly losing its luster.

So, how could the 1950's beauty bar be made relevant in the 21st Century? Unilever, which had absorbed Lever Brothers a decade earlier, decided rather than simply introduce a new glitzy marketing campaign, it was time to dig deeper – and actually re-examine what exactly beauty meant to women in this day and age. That was the kind of undertaking that would require a great deal of time, effort and money; the multinational corporation was willing to commit to a heavy investment in all three.

Unilever commissioned a global study on the uneasy relationship between women and their appearance. And this study was the real deal, based on quantitative data collected from a global study of 3,200 women, aged 18 to 64. StrategyOne, an applied research firm based in New York, managed the study in collaboration with Harvard University and the London School of Economics. Interviews were conducted across ten countries: the U.S., Canada, Great Britain, Italy, France, Portugal, Netherlands, Brazil, Argentina and Japan. And never once was the Dove brand mentioned or alluded to in any of these interviews.

In other words, this was not brand research – this was human research.

And the results were fairly shocking. Only 2% of the women respondents felt comfortable describing themselves as 'beautiful.' 40% of women 'strongly disagreed' that they were beautiful.[1] The conclusion of the study came down to this: 'The definition of beauty had become limiting and unattainable.'[2] That meant Dove had to figure out how to sell a beauty product to women who didn't think of themselves as beautiful.

The company's solution? Expand the definition of beauty.

That effort began with a revolutionary photo exhibit, 'Beyond Compare: Women Photographers on Real Beauty,' a show organized by Dove and Ogilvy & Mather. The showing featured work from world-famous female photographers showcasing so-called 'ordinary women,' photographed like models. In 2005, this concept expanded into a print campaign also centered on portraying real women with real bodies, but treating them as though they were professional models in print ads and photos.

This attention-getting approach generated such huge media conversations both in social media and on television talk shows that

---

1. "The Real Truth about Beauty: A Global Report" – Findings of the Global Study on Women, Beauty and Well-Being, September 2004, available at http://www.clubof amsterdam.com/contentarticles/52%20 Beauty/dove_white_paper_final.pdf
2. http://www.dove.us/Social-Mission/campaign-for-real-beauty.aspx

Dove's ad agency estimated it got 30 times the marketing value from the ad space it purchased. That success prompted a continuation and expansion of the campaign. In 2006, Dove produced several compelling videos chronicling the world's unrealistic expectations of female beauty – all of which went viral. One of them, 'Evolution,' alone garnered over 18 million views on YouTube.[3] Dove further cemented its commitment to this social issue by aligning itself with the Girl Scouts, the Boys and Girls Clubs of America and Girls Inc. to promote self-esteem in girls about their looks.

Dove's Real Beauty campaign continues to this day, attracting enormous media attention and creating heated controversy. Their Facebook page alone had 19 million 'likes.' According to Sharon MacLeod, vice president of Unilever North America Personal Care, "The conversation is as relevant and fresh today as it was 10 years ago, I believe we'll be doing this campaign 10 years from now."[4]

Why is she so sure about that? Perhaps because the former $200 million-a-year brand is now worth about $4 billion – purely as a result of the company transforming itself from an everyday soap seller into a Mission-Driven Brand.

If you've never understood what the power of a mission can do for a nuts-and-bolts business, the preceding Dove story illustrates what a difference it can make. If a fifty-year-old fading soap company can completely reinvigorate its image and become one of the most talked-about brands of our times – simply by taking on a mission that's more about society than marketing – it's hard to see why any other kind of business would be unable to do the same, no matter how old or seemingly set in its ways it happens to be.

Does that include your business?

Think about it. What if you were to become a Mission-Driven business? How might a mission transform both your brand and your business results? How might it attract a whole new base of customers and clients – as well as boost your profile and your prestige?

---

3. https://www.youtube.com/watch?v=iYhCn0jf46U
4. Bahadur, Nina. "Dove 'Real Beauty' Campaign Turns 10: How A Brand Tried To Change The Conversation About Female Beauty," The Huffington Post, January 21, 2014 http://www.huffingtonpost. com/2014/01/21/dove-real-beauty-campaign-turns-10_n_4575940.html

If you really want to beat the curve, becoming Mission-Driven can make that crucial difference and lift you above your competition. In this chapter, we're going to help you explore your Mission-Driven possibilities by revealing the three stages you must work through in order to put your specific mission into action. And remember, even if you already run a business, you can easily adapt it to a Mission-Driven one (in the same way Dove Soap did in the story that opened this chapter).

We uncovered these three stages through our work with more than 2000 clients at our agency. Our interest is always in helping them develop the potential of their businesses to the fullest. That's of course not an entirely altruistic impulse on our part – because, frankly, if our clients don't succeed, we don't succeed.

One of the easiest ways for us to set the foundation for our process is to relate it to a concept you may have already heard of. That concept is entitled 'The Golden Circle,' articulated in a world-famous TED talk given by ex-advertising executive Simon Sinek.[5] The basis of the Golden Circle is Sinek's analysis of the reason many of the world's most effective individuals and companies find such high levels of success. His research demonstrated that success is a result of 'Inside-Out' thinking – a progression from 'Why' to 'How' to, finally, 'What.'

Here's Sinek's graphic representation of this progression:

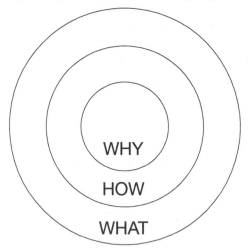

5. For more on the Golden Circle, Sinek's TED talk can be viewed at this link: http://www.ted.com/talks/simon_sinek_how_great_leaders_inspire_action?language=en

The successful people and companies Sinek profiles always start with the 'Why'; in other words, before they started out towards a major accomplishment, they keyed into their inner passions and what mattered to them most. Their next step was to figure out 'How' they were going to line up their life direction with those passions – and then, finally, they would take a look at 'What' they were going to do to bring all that to fruition.

How is that different from most people's approaches? According to Sinek, too many individuals instead start with their 'What,' leading them into lives with which they don't feel a real connection. These are the kinds of people that take a job simply to have a job and don't make enough of an effort to explore what they really want to do. Granted, we all have to do things to support ourselves, but when that short-term need dominates our long-term lives, we often dull the real individual power that comes from our intuition and true inner motivations.

What appeals to us about Sinek's model is it provides the perfect path for taking a personal mission from the theoretical to the practical. An idea isn't really worth a lot until you find a way to actually put it to work in the real world – and we've developed a process designed to do just that, and as you'll see, it aligns very well with Sinek's 'Why,' 'How' and 'What' progression.

Now, let's go more into detail about the three stages of our Action Process.

STAGE ONE: YOUR 'WHY'
DISCOVERING YOUR LIFE MISSION

This is where it all begins.

Your Life Mission lays the foundation of your Mission-Driven organization. It represents one or more aspects of what you care about the most – your deepest passion, your greatest talent and/or your biggest social concern. Your Life Mission is your greatest motivator to both dream and achieve.

Here are three historic figures who have readily identifiable Life

Missions that you're almost certainly already aware of:

- **Mother Theresa:** To continually help the poor and needy.
- **Mahatma Gandhi:** To fight for justice, freedom and dignity for all.
- **Steve Jobs:** A relentless drive to create and innovate with technology.

In the case of all three of the above individuals, most people immediately think of their Life Mission when they hear their names. It defined them more than anything else about them.

The right Life Mission will do the same for you. It will make you identifiable and memorable – as well as shape others' opinions of you. It will also draw supporters to your side and create a directed energy that helps you clear a strong and specific path. But your Life Mission will only succeed at all that if it comes from something strong and authentic within you.

The bottom line of your Life Mission is your 'Why.' It ties directly into your life motivations as well as your greatest enthusiasms in your dayto-day life.

It's what gives you *purpose*.

STAGE TWO: YOUR 'HOW'
FINDING THE VEHICLE TO ACTIVATE YOUR LIFE MISSION

If your Life Mission represents the idealistic 'Why' that motivates you, then your company or non-profit represents the practical *Vehicle* that becomes 'How' – the way you work towards your Life Mission in the real world.

For example, you might be someone who in general loves gourmet food – that's your Life Mission. But what do you do with that love – how do you fulfill your Life Mission? Do you open a restaurant? Become a chef? Or a food critic? The choice of vehicle for your Life Mission will most likely be made based on your other talents, interests, resources and opportunities.

More on that later. For now, let's take the three individuals whose Life Missions we just described – and talk about the vehicles they used to realize them.

• Mother Theresa decided her Life Mission to help the needy needed as its vehicle an infrastructure to enable her to help the impoverished on a global level. With that in mind, she founded the Missionaries of Charity, a Roman Catholic religious congregation, which currently consists of over 4,500 sisters and operates health clinics and programs for the disadvantaged in over 130 countries.

• Gandhi's Life Mission of justice and freedom drove him to lead India to gain independence from British rule. He used as his vehicle political power by working with the Indian Congress to build his national influence, and then, in turn, inspiring his countrymen to participate in mass protests demanding selfgovernance for India.

• Steve Jobs' Life Mission to innovate found its vehicle through the founding and running of Apple, and leading that corporation to release a steady stream of groundbreaking and ridiculously successful products.

In each case, an authentic Life Mission manifested itself in a vehicle that allowed the accomplishment of the mission. Your vehicle therefore, is your 'How' – it's how your Life Mission gets out of your brain and into the world.

STAGE THREE: YOUR 'WHAT'
DETERMINING YOUR ANNUAL CAMPAIGN

Rome wasn't built in a day. And you certainly can't accomplish a true Life Mission in 24 hours or less either. That's why you need to figure out 'What' to do with your vehicle to move towards your Life Mission in a thought-out step-by-step process.

Many people get caught up in the fact that they aren't able to visualize what their life or business will look like in 5, 10, 15, or even 20 years. While we absolutely think it's important to have long-term goals, we also don't want your inability to see the future (believe us, we can't either!) to keep you from getting started. Creating a succession of shortterm plans designed to take you closer to your ultimate ambitions also enables you to change up things more easily when the unexpected throws you for a loop. Because, as former boxer Mike Tyson once said, "Everybody has a plan until they get punched in the mouth." In life and business, we often get some blows we didn't expect, which is why we believe employing Annual Campaigns is the best ongoing strategy.

In our mind, every single calendar year a new Annual Campaign should be put into place that will enable a company or nonprofit to reach some significant benchmark in the effort to reach its Life Mission. This is where the rubber meets the road; practicality is the order of the day and a nuts-and-bolts approach must be found that everyone you work with can understand and get on board with.

If you've read or seen any of the numerous Steve Jobs' biographies, you know that this man rode herd on Apple execs and employees to deliver what he knew he wanted. From the iMac to iTunes to the iPod and the iPhone, he constantly provided an updated Annual Campaign to take the company to the next level. Now, he didn't specifically call it that, but there is a reason why Apple holds its Worldwide Developer Conference once a year; it's the same reason many other companies host annual gatherings and conferences. It's a whole lot easier to think in one year increments than it is to plot out a complete path towards a lifetime ambition.

From the Life Mission to the vehicle to a series of Annual Missions, the Mission-Driven process progresses from your innermost passions to incremental real-world stages that bring your Life Mission to life in a substantial and concrete way. Simply put, it's 'What' you need to do within your vehicle to reach your goals.

This, then, is our version of the Golden Circle we discussed earlier:

Life Mission | vehicle | Annual Campaigns

As the graphic illustrates, the Life Mission starts deep within you, from vital aspects of your identity (your 'Why'). This vehicle then helps you connect your Life Mission to the outside world through an infrastructure designed with that in mind (your 'How'). Finally, your Annual Campaigns are engineered to move you closer and closer to your

Life Mission through practical steps (your 'What'). In this progression, you start from a place of pure ideals – and finally discover how you can put them to work in a less-than-ideal society.

In our forthcoming book on Mission-Driven companies, you'll discover an Action Process we've developed which is designed to help you work through these three stages yourself in order to transform your business into a Mission-Driven one. In that book, you'll also discover the incredible advantages being Mission-Driven bestows on your business or nonprofit organization. It's a lot of valuable information we don't have the space to include here (that's why we had to write a whole book!) – but trust us when we tell you that becoming Mission-Driven, when done properly, always helps you redefine success!

About Nick

From the slums of Port au Prince, Haiti, with special forces raiding a sex-trafficking ring and freeing children, to the Virgin Galactic Space Port in Mojave with Sir Richard Branson, the 22-Time Emmy Award Winning Director/Producer, Nick Nanton, has become known for telling stories that connect. Why? Because he focuses on the most fascinating subject in the world: PEOPLE.

As a storyteller and Best-Selling Author, Nick has shared his message with millions of people through his documentaries, speeches, blogs, lectures, and best-selling books. Nick's book *StorySelling* hit *The Wall Street Journal* Best-Seller list and is available on Audible as an audio book. Nick has directed more than 60 documentaries and a sold out Broadway Show (garnering 43 Emmy nominations in multiple regions and 22 wins), including:

- *DREAM BIG: Rudy Ruettiger LIVE on Broadway*
- *Visioneer: The Peter Diamandis Story*
- *Rudy Ruettiger: The Walk On*
- *Operation Toussaint*
- *The Rebound*

Nick has shared the stage, co-authored books, and made films featuring:

- Larry King
- Dick Vitale
- Kenny Chesney
- Charles Barkley
- Coach Mike Krzyzewski
- Jack Nicklaus
- Tony Robbins
- Steve Forbes
- will.i.am
- Sir Richard Branson
- Dean Kamen
- Ray Kurzweil
- Lisa Nichols
- Peter Diamandis
......and many more

Nick specializes in bringing the element of human connection to every viewer, no matter the subject. He is currently directing and hosting the series: *In Case You*

Didn't Know (Season 1 Executive Produced by Larry King), featuring legends in the worlds of business, entrepreneurship, personal development, technology, and sports.

CHAPTER 5

"LOOKING FOR THE PONY"

BY SHARON PAPO

"Put you in a pile of sh*t and you'll look for the pony," quipped my mother-in-law, Patti, after I shared the hidden gift of slowing down on a sick day. For as long as my wife's mother has known me, I have been the eternal optimist. I took this acknowledgement of holding a positive outlook as a high compliment, because seeing the bright side didn't always come easy.

It all goes back to kindergarten. While my classmates effortlessly handled their scissors, I struggled during craft time. The deceptively simple task of cutting shapes, easily mastered by my peers, morphed into my personal Everest. Despite my right-handed teacher's best intentions, her techniques felt like an untranslatable dialect that left me disheartened.

In these tender early years, my left-handedness initially nudged me towards the false belief that I was innately flawed. "I just can't do it!" I screamed to my parents in a fit of frustration. That's when my right-handed parents offered me a much-needed paradigm shift. They told me that my left-handedness was not a deficit, but a distinctive trait that set me apart. They bought me left-handed scissors and gave me a different perspective that celebrated, rather than lamented, my deviation from the norm. Left-handed scissors: $2 at Target. Perspective shift: Priceless.

As I navigated my elementary school years, I was low in the social pecking order. I had few friends, and my inner voice began to morph from a whisper of self-doubt into a roar of self-criticism. At night, I found myself replaying my day's failures on the silver screen of my mind. Every recollection of a mistake or a cruel peer comment filled me with shame. Rehashing my 'darkest moments' intensified my insecurities, leading to many tear-filled sleepless nights.

As my negative beliefs intensified, compounded by the death of my beloved grandmother, I became trapped in my own mental quicksand. I started entertaining suicidal thoughts. I recall a moment standing in my kitchen, where I thought about hurting myself with our sharpest knife. At age 8, I was sent to weekly therapy and started taking antidepressants.

One of the people I confided in during my formative years was my cello teacher, Mrs. McBirney. Before my lesson began, she listened to me with a patient ear and an open heart. After I poured out my tribulations, she offered words of empathy and then redirected my attention by inquiring, "Now tell me what went right this week." That gentle request conveyed a profound wisdom that helped to shift my thoughts, focus, and energy. This improved my mood and got me present for our lesson. Beyond the cello's melodies, Mrs. McBirney taught me a poignant life lesson which I carried with me through my high school years and beyond: when we look for the good, we find it. My self-esteem grew along with my positive outlook and I was able to get off of the anti-depressants by the age of 13.

After college, I was hired as a health educator for incarcerated and homeless youth. Empowering these resilient teens amidst their considerable challenges was deeply rewarding. I poured my heart into my work, received outstanding evaluations, and exceeded our program goals. I fondly recall the heavily-tattooed teenage boy who sheepishly approached me to share that he was ready to make more positive choices based on the six-week class I had taught. It was a shocking blow when the successful program was terminated a few days later due to lack of funding.

My initial response was a mix of sadness and anxiety - sadness for the teens losing this crucial resource and anxiety for my financial stability. I found myself mulling over every possible difficulty and lying awake at night watching the greatest hits of my fears on my mind-TV.

After a week-long pity party, my wise father imparted a significant life lesson to me: we hold the power to assign meaning to each event in our lives. The choice was mine – to mourn an outcome that lay beyond my control or shape a more empowering narrative. In that moment, I intentionally chose to trust in my resilience. I started to reframe this unexpected turn as a catalyst propelling me towards my next professional adventure, in service of the greater good. I strategically positioned a reminder of this affirming message on my computer, refrigerator, and bathroom mirror.

Once I chose a more hopeful perspective, I found meaningful work again. I developed a new program called Puente: Building Bridges between Jews and Latinos. It was a program for college students to explore each other's culture, learn about discrimination and bias, and participate in service learning projects together. The participant evaluations were positive and all grant goals were met. Once again, I was dumbstruck when the program's grant funding was not renewed.

After being laid off a second time, I again spiraled into self-doubt and despair, but this time I managed to start rebounding after a few days. I started to journal and talk to my mentors and friends. I remembered that, while the layoffs and program closures were unchangeable facts, I was at choice about feeling like a victim. With a feeling like the universe was prompting me toward something bigger, I vowed to learn how to raise money so that wonderful organizations, like the ones I'd worked at, could maintain (and grow) their funding and continue to serve the community in more meaningful ways.

To move my career forward, I applied, and was accepted to, UC Berkeley's School of Social Welfare master's program. While I waited for my graduate program to begin, I was hired as a program coordinator at a respected Jewish youth leadership program. One of our retreats focused on the various aspects of diversity in our Jewish community. One program panel included a gay Jewish speaker who shared his heartfelt message of authenticity and acceptance. While the retreat was appreciated by the teen participants, the backlash was immediate and fierce when an irate parent started to organize to destroy our program. My supervisor pacified them by promising to cancel the diversity panel for future cohorts.

I had already started dating my future wife, but this ordeal reinforced my fears of rejection if I were to reveal that part of my identity. I was confronted with a seemingly impossible choice: my authenticity or my professional and communal standing. I dreamed of a future where I would work in, or even help build, a truly inclusive workplace. Despite the rejection from the conservative Jewish community that I grew up in, I felt called to be on a path towards positive change.

Feeling inspired to make a difference, I completed graduate school, dove into life/executive coaching training, found stellar mentors and took numerous intensive fundraising courses so I would never lose another position or valued program due to funding issues.

After graduate school, I was hired as the co-director of 3rd Street Youth Center and Clinic, an innovative multi-service adolescent health center in Bayview Hunters Point, an underserved neighborhood in San Francisco. Funding was tight and the space was tighter. Our vision quickly outgrew our small clinic and we knew that to truly serve the community, we would need a bigger space. I activated the fundraising knowledge I had learned and secured additional funds, doubling our annual fundraising. When a rare opportunity arose for us to move to a much larger building, I launched a successful capital campaign that helped to provide long-term stability for this important organization. At the ribbon cutting ceremony, I reflected back on the path to that moment. Losing jobs over funding issues early in my career turned out to be the best thing that could have happened for me and for 3rd Street Youth Center and Clinic.

I was proud of what we had built and, after 5 years, I was ready for a new challenge. I became the executive director of the Diversity Center, an LGBTQ+ Community Center. The critical nature of our work was clear. I will never forget the day that 'Chris' reluctantly walked through the door. 'Chris' shared that we were the first people she had ever 'come out' to. She was so afraid she would lose her job and be rejected by her family and her church, that she had decided to die by suicide - that day. She was literally on her way to the woods, with a gun in her trunk, to take her own life. 'Chris' happened to take a wrong turn onto our street and saw our rainbow flag out front. 'Chris' took it as a sign and entered our building for the first time. We surrounded 'Chris' with support – crisis resources, a therapist and camaraderie. 'Chris' insists her life today is due to that unforeseen detour.

We knew our community needed our organization strong. Once again, I put my fundraising skills into action. I worked with a team of staff and volunteers to quadruple the annual fundraising and execute a successful capital campaign which provided financial stability and established a forever home. The work was fulfilling, and when I left after 8 years, I was deeply honored that Jan. 12, 2021, was named Sharon Papo Day in the city of Santa Cruz 'in recognition of intersectional movement building and advocacy for the LGBTQ community.'

After twelve years as an executive director, I was ready for what was next. I thought I would work for an international company. I networked and applied (and applied and applied) and received zero job offers. Each rejection hurt. When that little voice in my head told me "you're not good enough," I intentionally talked back to that voice and reminded myself that good things lay ahead, even if I couldn't see it today.

I realized I needed to reconsider my professional direction. I had clarity that I stand for joy and wholeness for myself and others, and there are many ways that I can contribute to the world. With a friend's encouragement, I conducted 50 informational interviews. During my 50th conversation, I was encouraged to apply to be a capital campaign fundraising consultant. I applied, got hired, and realized that I really enjoyed the work. I got to show up as a strategist, cheerleader, and help people address their own toxic blocks around money while they ran a transformational fundraising campaign.

This experience inspired me to launch Indigo Skies Consulting, my boutique firm specializing in executive coaching and fundraising consulting. This work was fulfilling, and I also felt I had more to do for the LGBTQ+ community. I co-founded a second company, LGBTQ eLearning, with Dr. Cornell Verdeja-Woodson, where we co-created an engaging self-paced eLearning course called *Building LGBTQ+ Inclusive Workplaces.*

The 'rejections' from those previous jobs guided me on my current path where I get to be of even greater service to more people and worthy causes, while having a better work/life balance. It is an honor to be able to guide and empower individuals to grow into transformative, effective and inclusive leaders.

Reflecting on my journey, my current successful and fulfilling path would not have materialized without the invaluable and hard lessons learned during my early days. Enduring the weight of losing jobs and witnessing worthy programs dissolve due to insufficient funding – twice, compelled me to delve deeply into the realm of fundraising to help community-based organizations have the resources they need to make the impact they are committed to. Enduring the attack after the diversity panel inspired me to co-found the company *LGBTQ eLearning* to help companies learn the skills to create inclusive workplaces. These transformative experiences paved the way for my current trajectory, but I would not have gotten here without the heavy lifting I did around my mindset.

Ultimately, we can choose if our minds are a source of empowerment or self-sabotage. We each have the power to improve our life outlook. It's not easy, but with practice and determination, it is absolutely possible. Our brains process 70,000 thoughts per day. We don't have to believe all of them! We don't have to be victims of our thoughts.

If you want to change your thoughts, the first thing to do is to notice which thoughts are causing you pain. Once you are aware of the negative thought, you can ask yourself:

- Is this thought even true?
- Would I say this to my friend?
- Is this thought serving me?

A gratitude practice became one of the easiest and most powerful ways for me to improve my thoughts. Taking time each day to intentionally focus on what I appreciate and what is working in my life brings my attention to the positive aspects. Writing a daily thank you note has been one of my favorite ways of taking time to be grateful and making someone else's day too.

If this all sounds pollyannaish to you, I will share that I don't believe that 'everything happens for a reason.' There are a lot of horrifying things in our world, and I can't and won't believe that these incredible hardships are divinely meant to be. A positive and hopeful frame of mind doesn't alter the harsh realities of poverty, illness, climate disasters, xenophobia, broken hearts, and so much more, but it helps us confront the hardships and resiliently navigate through them.

I have learned to embrace a positive mindset. It's an intentional choice every day. If I can do it, I know in every cell in my body that you can too. Just like learning to play a musical instrument or developing any specific skill set, it takes commitment and practice, but it's worth it.

At some point, we will all find ourselves in a metaphorical pile of sh*t. When you find yourself there, I hope you choose to look for the lesson, the growth, the metaphorical pony. It will always bring you more joy than focusing on the flies and the muck. We each have only one unique and precious life.

How do you want to experience yours?

About Sharon

Sharon Papo is a trailblazing executive coach, consultant, and trainer who is known for her positivity, genuine warmth, and sparkle. As the visionary Founder and CEO of Indigo Skies Consulting, Sharon has propelled numerous small and mid-size community-based organizations to strengthen their boards and surpass even their loftiest fundraising goals, by collectively raising well over $100 million dollars.

Sharon possesses an extraordinary talent for guiding her clients beyond the mental and emotional barriers that often hinder their fundraising success. Her expertise lies in orchestrating major gifts and capital campaigns, and transforming her clients' aspirations into tangible, awe-inspiring achievements.

In a powerful collaboration with Dr. Cornell Verdeja-Woodson, Sharon co-founded LGBTQ eLearning, a company that has received widespread acclaim for its flagship self-paced eLearning course *'Building LGBTQ+ Inclusive Workplaces.'* This eCourse serves as a guiding light, fostering understanding, compassion, and helping to create a greater sense of belonging in workplaces across various sectors. Sharon is known for delivering powerful keynotes, engaging fireside chats, and skillfully moderating LGBTQ+ employee panels.

Sharon's academic journey reflects her unwavering commitment to making the world a better place. With a master's degree from UC Berkeley's School of Social Welfare and a license as a clinical social worker (LCSW), she possesses the compassion and skills needed to create meaningful growth for individuals, teams, and companies. Additionally, Sharon earned a B.A. in Gender Studies from the University of California, Santa Cruz, and a Diversity and Inclusion certificate from Cornell University. This educational background forms the foundation of her holistic approach to fostering inclusivity.

The impact of Sharon's work was officially recognized by the City of Santa Cruz, CA, when they declared January 12, 2021 'Sharon Papo Day,' to honor Sharon's intersectional movement building and advocacy for the LGBTQ+ community.

Sharon lives in California where she shares her life with her wife and two energetic, lovable kids that fuel her drive to create a world where everyone can thrive, regardless of who they are.

To embark on a journey of personal and professional growth with Sharon, reach out to her at:

- sharon@indigoskiesconsulting.com.

You can learn more at:

- SharonPapo.com
- LGBTQeLearning.com

CHAPTER 6

THE JOURNEY FROM POWERLESSNESS TO EMPOWERMENT

BY ROBERT BEATTY

Once a model of discipline with a 13-year military stint and flourishing businesses, I quickly became the face of destruction. Early success, wealth, and admiration defined me, but trauma and personal downfalls marked the beginning of my descent. Alcohol became my refuge, and soon my life paralleled a crashing 747—unyielding, total chaos.

In the span of a year, alcoholism dismantled my life. My family left me, my businesses went bankrupt, and legal troubles multiplied. The memory of my wife's departure is still fresh, where I, intoxicated and deluded, normalized my pitiful existence. The comfort of my home turned to a dingy condo, and even that was stripped away as I struggled to hold onto anything stable.

When utilities were cut off, I told myself, "Who needs them? I have alcohol." When I lost my home, I believed my car was enough—until that too was repossessed. I assured myself things would change, but they worsened. For over a year, my days merged into a haze of acquiring money, primarily to quench my alcoholic thirst.

Two DUI arrests, including one that destroyed a borrowed truck, left me truly homeless. I was a specter haunting Salt Lake City's streets, seeking refuge in bug-infested hotels, constantly chasing the solace of alcohol. I was convinced that my children had written me off for dead, and I regularly wondered if I had hit my lowest. But each day seemed to challenge that thought.

My existence centered around procuring and consuming alcohol. Days were marked by the constant balancing act of obtaining just enough funds for a bottle and a place to sleep. I stooped to begging, using my veteran status as a plea, and relied on strangers' charity. Sometimes, I'd sleep outdoors, clutching a bottle.

One particularly chilling memory stands out: a former colleague, not recognizing the gaunt, ragged figure I'd become, pityingly handed me money. My previous 190-pound frame had dwindled to 140 pounds, disguising my identity. Yet, in my deluded state, this was just another 'acceptable low'. The cycle continued, each day ensuring just enough for shelter and a cheap bottle. Whenever I believed things couldn't get worse, life proved me wrong. The phrase 'acceptable new low' became a constant refrain.

Anger consumed me—anger toward the world, toward God, and most of all, toward myself. I felt cornered, desperate, and determined not to seek help from anyone, no matter the circumstances. I was convinced that no one cared.

Christmas that year, without a shred of doubt, stands as one of the most arduous trials I have ever been through. The significance of Christmas in my life had always been monumental, a cherished cornerstone of my existence. The joy of doting upon my beloved children, crafting moments of bliss, was a privilege I held dear.

In the abyss of my existence, I found myself alone, homeless, and scraping by within the confines of a meager, threadbare hotel room. Aware of the dangerous nature of my affliction, my own mother, wise beyond measure, withheld any form of monetary aid, knowing all too well that it would only fuel the fire that consumed me.

However, in a final flicker of hope, she helped me salvage a semblance of Christmas spirit, not for myself, but for my children. She entrusted me with the use of a department store credit card, which happened to be across the way from my hotel. With the fragile card clutched tightly,

I ventured out to procure meager offerings for my precious children. In the face of their modesty, it was but a droplet in an ocean of desires, yet it brought me a fleeting serenity, a momentary break from the suffocating grip of despair.

I reached out, leaving messages and texts, blindly hoping for a reunion during the holiday season. It had not dawned upon me, clouded by my own anguish, that they sought refuge from the demon that ravaged my mind and body. As the eve of Christmas descended, an insurmountable weight of desolation crushed my spirit. The poignant images of my beloved children nestled within the bosom of a loving family, while I languished alone in a desolate hotel room, drowning my sorrows in an elixir of intoxication to numb the searing ache that gnawed at my very core.

And then, a glimmer pierced the shroud of darkness. It was a call from my daughter, extending an invitation to share a moment, a respite from my despair. With newfound hope pulsating through my veins, I hastily gathered their gifts, trembling, sick from alcohol withdrawal, praying for salvation.

As we headed to the movie theater, there was a glimmer of hope that we could find some unity amidst the chaos. But my sorry state betrayed me, casting a shadow of discomfort over our fragile reunion. Even beneath their forced smiles, it was clear that my drunkenness and illness burdened their tender hearts. With the exchange of gifts and a heavy silence, my daughter bid me farewell, leaving my shattered dreams behind in that lonely hotel room.

In that moment, everything unraveled, and the symphony of emotional and physical agony echoed through the depths of my soul. I lay on the bed, curled up in a ball, tormented cries escaping my trembling lips. Anguished, I pleaded with a higher power, "Why, God? Why have you abandoned me? How much more must I bear?" Desperate to numb the overwhelming sorrow, I sought solace in the deceptive embrace of a half-gallon bottle filled to the brim with vodka. I surrendered to its alluring oblivion, allowing it to consume me.

In the dead of the night, I awakened, hearing my friends imploring me to save my life from my bedside. I soon realized these were hallucinations, but their voices remained, urging me to seek help. Overcome by a severe withdrawal episode, I panicked, believing death was imminent. Instead of heeding my retired nurse mother's advice to hospitalize myself, I chose to drown the withdrawal symptoms with more alcohol. The consequences were dire. While speaking to her, I succumbed to a violent seizure and heart failure, my last breath echoing through the phone, causing her to promptly dial 911.

There, doctors explained my critical condition: liver and kidney issues, severe internal bleeding, and a heart that had temporarily stopped. When asked about suicidal thoughts, I bitterly asked for guidance on how to end it all. Surely, I had hit rock bottom. Yet, I was still clinging on.

During my nine-day detox, the doctor informed me of my irreparable liver damage, my failing kidneys, fluid that was building up around my heart, and internal bleeding due to esophagitis. I pleaded for a solution only to be met with the harsh reality: there was no fix, no hope of a liver transplant, no reprieve from the unstoppable march towards death. His final advice to me was to 'pray'. Thus, I had encountered an unacceptable new low that, finally, I could not accept.

In that pivotal moment of my life, lying in the hospital bed, I was struck with a profound realization that my life on this earth had just ended. The gravity of my drinking problem became undeniably clear. As the next two days stretched on, I found myself engulfed in a sea of physical and emotional pain, consumed by anger and withdrawal. My fear of death turned to a fear of living another minute in the pain and suffering of this world. The weight of my actions and the devastating impact on my family and children weighed heavily on my heart. I felt utterly defeated, broken, and overwhelmed by a deep desire to escape it all, even if it meant giving up on life itself. I couldn't fathom facing my children or family after what I had put them through. The shame and guilt gnawed at my soul.

Amidst the agony and sleepless nights, an unexpected visitor appeared in my hospital room. Whether it was a figment of my imagination, a dream, or something more, I can't say for certain. This mysterious figure exuded confidence and charm, captivating me with a charismatic presence. He posed uncomfortable questions about the immortality

I sought, offering an alluring but sinister alternative solution. I grew increasingly uneasy as the conversation progressed, sensing that this individual was not what he seemed. He insidiously whispered that I had no one to turn to, that he was the only one left who loved me, and that he held all the answers and everything I desired. Discomfort turned to alarm, and I demanded his immediate departure. "Okay, I'll be around," he responded, leaving a lingering sense of unease.

What happened next took me by surprise. Overwhelmed by pain and desperation, I tumbled off the bed and fell to my knees, crying out in a prayer that was more heartfelt and impassioned than anything I had ever uttered before. It was an outward expression of grief, a plea for forgiveness from my children, and a desperate call for divine intervention. "Please God, help me! Please, help me!" I beseeched, pouring out my anguish and surrendering to a force greater than myself. I had reached the bottom. The unacceptable new low. At that moment, I finally let go of my pride, ego, my illusions of control, and delusional image of myself, my stubborn resistance. Defeated, alone, and stripped of all pretenses, I was at the mercy of my circumstances.

Physically and emotionally drained, I pleaded with God, abandoning all resistance, and declaring my willingness to be taken from this world. "I give up. Please, God, please take me. I can't bear to live another moment of this anguish. I don't know what you want from me. Just take me now!" Exhausted and broken, I cried myself to sleep on the cold hospital floor.

When I awoke the next morning, my eyes met the gaze of a vibrant bluebird perched on a windowsill. In that moment, an inexplicable shift occurred. All the pain, anger, depression, anxiety, loneliness, and fear that had consumed me vanished. It was as if a divine presence had intervened, cradling me in a profound sense of love, peace, and serenity. The weight of my burdens had somehow been lifted, replaced by a newfound awareness that someone had gently guided me back to the bed during the night when I was too weak to stand. I finally grasped the true meaning of powerlessness.

On this life altering, unforgettable morning, God was doing for me what I could no longer do for myself. I recognized that my life had been devoid of a connection with God. I had been running away from him for so long, not understanding that his spiritual presence was what I desperately needed in my life. God held all the power, and I, in my surrender, finally accepted my own powerlessness.

Four days later, against the advice of medical professionals, I mustered the strength to leave the hospital. I reached out to my mother, humbly asking if I could seek refuge in her home for a while, yearning for a haven to embark on my healing journey. From the moment I awakened that morning in that hospital room, I felt a palpable presence of God surrounding me. A profound sense of peace enveloped my being, and I knew deep in my soul that this was the turning point, the beginning of a transformative journey toward a life of sobriety.

In the days that followed, I embarked on a path of recovery unlike anything I had ever experienced. Every step I took was guided by a newfound faith and an unwavering trust in a power greater than myself and the unmistakable conviction of my own powerlessness. I immersed myself in prayer and meditation, seeking solace and guidance in the divine. It was the strength and resilience I needed to confront the challenges ahead.

As I settled into my mother's home, I embraced the healing process with a renewed determination. I was very sick and knew that I had a long way to go. I surrounded myself with a supportive network of loved ones who understood the gravity of my journey and stood by my side unconditionally. Together, we created a space of understanding, compassion, and accountability—a sanctuary where I could share my fears, insecurities, and triumphs.

Each day became a testament to my commitment to sobriety. I no longer relied on self-medication to drown out the pain or escape the reality of my past. Instead, I confronted my demons head-on, working through the deep-rooted issues that fueled my addiction. With the support of a mentor and the guidance of recovery programs, I delved into the Twelve Steps, examining my shortcomings, and making amends to those that I had harmed.

It was during this transformative process that I realized the true meaning of acceptance and surrender. It wasn't a sign of weakness, but rather an act of courage—a conscious choice to relinquish control and place my faith in something greater than myself. I acknowledged my powerlessness over my addiction, and embraced the notion that my journey to lasting recovery required a spiritual awakening. With humility and a newfound sense of humility, I opened myself to the possibility of change.

With time, the wounds of the past started to heal, and I embarked on the process of rebuilding my life. I mended broken relationships, making amends to those I had harmed and worked diligently to rebuild trust. I sought professional help to address the underlying issues of mental illness that contributed to my addiction, attending therapy sessions and participating in support groups to gain valuable insights and coping mechanisms.

After fully recovering, I returned to Purdue University to pursue a Master's Degree in Addiction Psychology. I've since become a prominent figure in the recovery community. I've written four books: *How Free Do You Want To Be*, *A Guide To Spiritual Awakening*, *The Business Of Healing*, and *Desperation Of A Dying Man*. I'm also the co-founder of New U Recovery in Park City, Utah, founder of The Retreat At Zion in Rockville, Utah, Zion Recovery outpatient services and Zion Healing Centers.

Zion Healing has grown remarkably due to our unwavering commitment, resulting in 20 area expansions and the establishment of 60 clinics, both operational and in the pipeline, across the country.

Through these centers, our educational endeavors, our special programs for Veterans, and direct mentorship, I've had the honor of guiding hundreds of individuals on their path to overcoming addiction and mental health adversities.

Today, I stand as a testament to the power of surrender and the transformative nature of recovery. My experience serves as a reminder that hitting rock bottom was not the end, but rather the catalyst for a profound spiritual awakening and a life filled with purpose and meaning. By surrendering my will to a higher power, I discovered a strength within myself that I never knew existed—a strength that continues to guide me on the path of sobriety, serenity, peace, and freedom.

About Robert

Robert Beatty has *personal knowledge* of the pain and destruction caused by these issues. He has an amazing story of spiritual awakening, redemption, and *a journey to full recovery* from chronic depression and mental illness.

Early in his adult life, he accomplished a successful 13-year military enrollment and then moved on to a film and television career, financing and producing numerous productions and films. Along with the success came the stresses of running a publicly-traded corporation, producing, financing, managing employees, successes, and failures.

By age 46, these issues had taken everything from Robert including his marriage, children, business, and home. Alcohol had also taken its toll on his health. In 2010, Robert found himself homeless, physically, mentally and emotionally broken, and hospitalized. He was told by doctors that he would not live out the day, that his liver had failed completely, and there were no other options available. Finding himself homeless, broken, defeated, and standing on death's door, he experienced the miracle of a spiritual awakening and the power of a higher power for the first time in his life.

Robert fully recovered and went back to College at Purdue University, pursuing his master's degree of Psychology in Addiction. He is active in the recovery community.

Robert is the author of several books on addiction and recovery, including *How Free Do You Want To Be, A Guide To Spiritual Awakening, The Business Of Healing,* and *Desperation Of A Dying Man*. Robert is the co-founder of New U Recovery residential inpatient treatment center near Park City, Utah, founder of The Retreat At Zion residential inpatient treatment center in Rockville, Utah, Zion Recovery outpatient services in St. George, Utah. Zion Healing Centers are a nationwide provider of behavioral and mental health services with 20 area developments and over 60 franchise clinics open and in development stages throughout the U.S.A.

In 2023, Robert launched the Zion Healing Development Corp and Veterans Initiative which will build inpatient and outpatient treatment centers within proximity of US military bases, VA hospitals and rural underserviced areas to provide treatment for substance use disorders and mental health services for Veterans in need.

He is a public speaker and regular on talk shows, radio broadcasts, podcasts, and was featured on the cover and feature article of *Recovery Today Magazine* in 2018. Through the years, Robert has assisted countless individuals to overcome mental health issues and addiction through his treatment centers, education, and mentorship. He is the father of five children and six grandchildren.

Connect with Robert:

- facebook.com/rcord63

CHAPTER 7

SUCCESS COMES ONLY FROM WITHIN

BY KIERSTEN BLEST

By my estimation, I had taken a wrong turn and hiked the wrong path for two thousand, one hundred, and ninety days. Attempting to fit in with a company in which I did not belong, I was following instructions for advancement that fit like they were shoes two sizes too small, speaking in advanced corporate jargon, dressing like someone I wasn't, editing my opinions, constantly worrying about what other people thought, squeezing out words of "I'm fine," and "Everything's good!" while shielding the truth. This was all to gain approval, feel good enough, and achieve success by accomplishing more with fewer mistakes, so I could safeguard my job to pay my bills and raise my son while keeping myself emotionally safe in the process.

It was a jam-packed daily agenda.

And, like most people I knew, my agenda was peppered with more agendas. There was the *Do the Right Thing Agenda*, driven by what others expected, wanted, or requested, even when I didn't have the available time, interest, or energy. It involved following through on commitments I should never have made in the first place, maintaining longstanding relationships that were no longer fun, saying yes to events when I was running on empty, and accepting every invitation for weddings, baby showers, and barbeques that came my way, even if I barely knew the person.

The Maintain the Marriage Agenda, rewritten at least five times, ultimately evolved into one that consisted of strained couple's therapy sessions and forced date nights on top of vanilla conversations about *how was your day* and *what we should do for dinner* before sleeping separately in a house of stone cold silence. It required staying together long past our expiration date for reasons that barely made sense then and make zero sense now when I look back at the precious time wasted.

And, of course, there was the *Family Agenda*. By that, I mean my family of origin, which is a story in and of itself. But for now, suffice it to say, it was more of a mandate than a memo and one so utterly demanding that it regularly derailed all other agendas without apology, remorse, or regret.

But the kingpin of all was the *Agenda of Career*, not only because it occupied most of my time but because it un-neatly overlapped with the *Agenda of Employee.* The reality was that no matter what position I held, how many people I oversaw, or how much money I earned, I worked for someone else. That meant I merged into their agenda, from eight o'clock in the morning until whenever, five solid days a week, minus only a handful of holidays and overdue vacations... most of which I worked anyway. That was the typical corporate culture back then, and it was a standard upheld by those who desired to get ahead, which I did.

So, whatever required goals were assigned became default priorities. I chased each one, even when it was unrealistic or made no sense because there was no connection to personal or company goals.

The truth is that even though reaching these goals fulfilled provided momentary feelings of happiness, I quickly learned that the more I achieved, the more others expected. I moved up and across organizations more times than I can count, often without being asked and at times without additional pay. There was a widely-accepted belief that receiving more work, broader scope, and greater responsibility represented a form of recognition and reward. I bought into this concept early in my career, but the truth is that each move created more stress while taking time from other areas of my life, which never felt like a reward to me.

And each time I sprinted across a corporate bridge or climbed a corporate ladder, I chased more goals, more significant titles, and larger teams while growing more despondent. The feel-good feelings of achieving whatever was next lasted only a short time because there was always something new to chase.

It's not surprising when you think about how we grow up. We're on the move from our earliest years, chasing milestones we don't even remember, like crawling, walking, and riding a bike without training wheels. We chase losing our first tooth, a new school year, each summer vacation, and the next birthday and holiday. We chase team victories, individual awards, our first kiss, our first love, high-school graduation, and acceptance into college before chasing our first adult job, marriage, and maybe having children while chasing higher salaries, promotions, and bigger offices. If we trade in the corporate world for entrepreneurship, we chase new clients, more revenue, and more profit. We chase losing weight, bigger houses, fancier cars, and whatever else will make us feel successful, accomplished, and fulfilled.

And then we watch with anticipation as our children grow and begin chasing many of the same goals, in much the same way, while we cheer them on from the sidelines. And the whole process of chasing a future event repeats through the next generation. At the same time, we move into our later years, push towards our finish line, and chase retirement with enough money tucked away so that we can finally stop chasing.

During that time in my life, I didn't question why I continued to sling-shot myself out my front door each morning for a job that no longer brought me joy, only to drag myself back home every evening to a hollow relationship. I didn't question why I felt compelled to make choices dictated by stacks of agendas or why they mattered in the first place. I didn't question why I wasn't paying attention to my quality of life or when the passion I once felt every day disappeared.

I didn't question much for those two thousand one hundred ninety days until I reached a collision of crossroads that woke me up, They woke me up with the reminder that I had free will, the world was at my feet, nothing was set in stone, and I could instantly decide to stop hiking in the wrong direction, choose a different path and feel differently about my life.

Have you ever heard someone tell you to *do what you want to do, be who you want to be, follow your dreams*, or *do what makes you happy?* They sound like words of encouragement. They read like a simple formula for success. They sound acceptable, especially in the context of work and career. It feels like it should be easy to live this way.

But not everyone grows up hearing words of encouragement or with unwavering support, and even for those that do, creating the life you want and defining success in a way that aligns with who you are isn't as easy as it sounds.

Many of us grow up adopting definitions of success shaped by our environments, including family, friends, society, and even the media. For me, success looked like graduating from college, working for a stable company, working long hours while starting a family, advancing my career, saving money, and ensuring I was tending to others' needs. Granted, it took me far by most definitions, but there came a point where multiple parts of my life became stagnant. It was a clear signal to let go of my conventional thinking and definition of success and finally construct my own.

I quickly discovered it wasn't an overnight task.

The first step is understanding how you came to believe what you believe in the first place. From there, it's about examining your values and diving into your identity. These are three essential components that dictate our choices. Sometimes, this is the most challenging work because even though many people feel they have a strong sense of self, they don't always see the truth of who they are. But when we understand how our identity is formed and how it's affected by our experiences with other people, the perceptions that others hold of us, and various cultural influences, we realize that discovering who we are is a process. And, within that process, you'll uncover what success means to you.

Once that's done, you can create goals to help you achieve what you want.

There are already loads of books and resources available that focus on achieving goals. Most offer prescribed steps like defining your outcome, taking action, changing habits, shifting your mindset, staying motivated, and responding to feedback, all of which are necessary. But if success were as simple as this blueprint suggests, most people would already have exactly what they want.

As a Master Success Coach with more than twenty-five years of corporate and coaching work, I can tell you that most people *don't* have everything they want, and most people admit they are experiencing lack in at least one area of their life.

I've worked with some who are thriving both personally and professionally while still aspiring for more. But I've encountered many more people who are struggling, burned out, dissatisfied with their jobs, unfulfilled in their relationships, or experiencing distress in some area of their life. While they're usually clear on what they want, whether it's more clients in their business, a bigger job, better health, a romantic relationship, more money, more work/life balance, or more *success*, they generally don't understand why they're not getting the results they want when, in their own words, they're doing everything *right*.

There are common threads you can't overlook if you want to succeed. Most importantly, you must live a life you choose to create instead of allowing others to influence your choices. Not sometimes, but *all the time*, with one-hundred percent commitment.

This is where many people get stuck. Because once we consciously choose our terms rather than accepting the terms of others by default, we generally meet resistance. The thing to know about resistance is that it exists in many forms and on various levels. It can be external through our friends, family, environment, and society. It can be internal through our thoughts and emotional energy. It can even exist at the level of our soul, which we experience through our intuition and higher knowing.

When I eliminated my mental agendas, I faced internal resistance. There was no longer anyone or anything to blame when things didn't go my way. Lousy luck, wrong timing, drawing the short straw, and others refusing to change were no longer excuses for my circumstances and discontent. It would have been easy to stop right there because the idea of having that much power over my life was terrifying. Yet, at the same time, it was utterly liberating.

Like many people who choose to divorce, resistance showed up through family and friends. I was somehow disappointing people who lived thousands of miles away. Everyone had an opinion; some told me I was making the wrong decision, a few went so far as to tell me I wasn't thinking about my son, while others shared stories of how they personally *hung in there when times were tough.* There was even a gathering of senior family members who felt compelled to help me get back on track and stop acting selfishly, while they practically ordered me to *stick it out.*

I didn't bend.

I knew that the advice of my family was rooted in their steadfast belief that divorce is wrong, a belief I once half-held but for very different reasons. While their belief was based on religious doctrine and a collective set of values, I knew mine was tied to my belief that divorce meant I wasn't good enough, which connected to my identity.

While my belief about divorce changed over the years as my sense of identity shifted, my family's belief remained constant; neither was wrong, and both were equally right. We all hold our own truths and have the power to change them at any time. I no longer associate divorce with failure. Instead, I defined failure for myself as a refusal to take action to change and own my circumstances.

When I launched my own business, I was clear on my values, my definition of success and how I wanted to feel. Yet I had my own business coach who spent multiple sessions attempting to convince me that I needed to become a content creator, host an online community, hop on social media, and author a solo book. It felt like it was a one-size-fits-all formula that didn't at all fit with me.

Even when I shared with a few professional colleagues that I would write this chapter, more than one suggested I leverage AI. While more and more people are generating content using AI, especially in the coaching arena, I also know that authenticity is my **number one** core value, so this would never work for me! But this quick story does illustrate another form of resistance that is easy to catch. You can quickly determine if you're trying to do something out of alignment with who you are; it will feel heavy, much like pushing a boulder uphill.

Resistance always has the potential to surface and can sting when it comes through as criticism or judgment. But in my experience, that doesn't come from people who are already fulfilled with their life and creating their own success.

Some people will fade off, some may try to bring you back down because this is because they are a better match for the prior version of you. Please don't let this make you question your commitment to yourself. Our environments directly reflect who we are at any given moment, so as you rise, your environment will rise. It can be no other way for this is the Universal Law of Vibration.

And as you continue to rise to your next level of success, creating life in your own way and reaching your goals on your own terms, I can only begin to describe for you what is waiting on the other side.

You going to discover an incredible sense of unwavering freedom, spaciousness, and inner peace that exists no matter what's happening around you. You'll move into a profound state of balance, replacing old stress and overwhelm.

And, with each step, you'll begin to expand into the highest expression of yourself, creating happier and more fulfilling relationships with all those around you and, most importantly, with yourself.

About Kiersten

Kiersten Blest is a Board Certified Master Success Coach, Master Practitioner of NLP, and a Certified Practitioner of Soul Realignment®, EFT, and Quantum Human Design™. She is a graduate of Bentley University with a BS in Business Management and has a long-standing career in Global Human Resources and Executive Coaching with Fortune 100 companies.

Kiersten is widely recognized for her expertise in helping individuals and small business owners figure out what makes them naturally successful, get clarity on their goals, and then unravel old ways of being and thinking that no longer serve their happiness and success.

She's known for her unique ability to quickly identify the root cause of resistance and her unique approach of blending science with energetic and spiritual insights.

She also co-authored the #1 Best Selling Book, *Becoming Positively Awesome* in 2023.

Originally from the Northeast, Kiersten resides in South Carolina with her son and amazing life partner, whom she's been blessed to know for more than forty-five years.

Learn more at:

- www.KierstenBlest.com

CHAPTER 8

LEAVE AND BECOME

BY ARMAND DJAGUEU

PART 1

DEVELOPING A MINDSET FOR TRUSTWORTHINESS AND PROSPERITY

Three years ago, a friend pawned his car to lend $1500 to me. Today, I own and manage a company with over $5 million revenue in the financial services sector. In keeping with the theme of this book, *Success Redefined* with Jack Canfield, I would say that trustworthy is the first capital in business, and I would have a lot to say about it.

Since childhood, I have always had the ambition to work for just five years and create my company. That is how my former General Manager and I created our own company on March 19, 2019, because of the company's poor performance due to the dissensions within management. Once created, the outgoing Managing Director didn't want me as a partner but rather as an employee with the position of Deputy General Manager.

After the General Manager had resigned, the directors offered me to replace him, but I categorically refused. I decided to leave the company, but short of money, I returned to work with the objective of reorienting my career.

CHALLENGES

- **The passage to the judicial police**
  Once at the office, an internal financial audit had been initiated. I refused to produce some documents for my own security and I was prosecuted for fictitious dividend payments. I then had to present the proper documentation to get out of this situation and my director was very angry with me.

In my defence, I asked my boss how could management actions that had been taken with the agreement of the Board of Directors be questioned. I took the opportunity to ask him if he would trust me in the future. These few words were enough to calm him down, but a few days later I was being disciplined.

- **The disciplinary sanction**
  I received a letter informing me of the withdrawal of my company vehicle, something that I refused.

- **The bargaining chip**
  I knew that the outcome of the audit was intended to affect the outgoing Director General. I also knew that my position allowed me to expose the truth, but by doing so, I would get myself in trouble. So, I had to find a bargaining chip.

For this, I made a contract instead with God. I undertook to bring out the whole truth to exonerate the outgoing Director and to help the parties find a compromise, and I undertook to do everything in my power to preserve the continuity of the company. As counterpart, God helped me leave the company and find my own way.

Staying Focused And Unflappable Helped Restore Confidence

I was doing my job properly to bring out the truth and to guarantee the continuity of the company. I had played this role so brilliantly that the situation was confusing for my two bosses. Trustworthy again, I was promoted to the position of Group Strategic Planner. But it was a sanctioned promotion with no salary increase.

THE TIPPING POINT

Before my resignation, because I refused both propositions of my two bosses, a friend asked why I could not become an investment banker.

THE REINVENTION

I started deconstructing the job of an investment banker, starting with support services aimed at equipping investment banks with appropriate management software, consulting services, and business training in securities management.

After two weeks, I had mastered the legal framework for the management of dematerialized securities operations and the information system on the requirements needed to ensure the technical reliability and security of processing and operations. I knew so much to the point that I had structured a commercial offer that offered software supply services for custodians (which I did not yet have). This was designed to support the bank in the organization and implementation of the integrated information system for management, accounting and custody of dematerialized Securities in order to meet the expectations of the supervisory bodies for dematerialization, and the management of Securities transactions.

I created my company and signed three contracts worth $66,000 with some multinational companies without being asked to demo the software. These companies took no risk. I was under the pain of a penalty of $10,000 per company; I had to obtain the certificate of conformity within 45 days before receiving the first franc.

FROM $60 TO $5 MILLION IN JUST 3 YEARS

With $60 all in, and despite the reluctance of those close to me, I used a promotion without a salary increase as an excuse to resign on February 5, 2020 and it cost me my fiancée, and many long-time friends.

A friend pawned his car for me to borrow $1,500, which allowed me, within one month, to deliver the first services for which I had made commitments and I received an advance of $30,000. It was enough to rent new offices and recruit developers to finalize the necessary software.

Today, Global Asset Cameroon is the reference in the OHADA environment as a support structure for financial market actors. This was for the supply of software for managing transactions on dematerialized securities and includes training and transfer of skills in the professions of brokerage firms, mutual fund organizations, custodians, and a management company with 22 employees who maintain more than 180 customers' accounts and protect more than 6,000 shareholders' rights.

We have already supported our clients in dematerializing and securing Transferable Securities for the equivalent of 1 billion dollars. In Africa, we have already been invited to share our expertise at more than 14 conferences.

THE REASONS FOR SUCCESS

Qualified human resources are rare in this field, so we have chosen to recruit people without any professional experience but who want to learn. We had a 5-year business plan based on a strategy of diversification of activities combining jobs in:

- Software development
- Custodial Account Holders of Securities
- Investment Banks
- Mutual Fund organization management companies.

We have identified the key skills needed to deploy each of the activities and have classified them into several Grades ranging from A to G to structure a career plan for each employee in each of the specific areas.

They all started in the apprenticeship grade, and each time they changed levels, this automatically implied for us the launching of the activities in the corresponding job. Today, in the first business, which is the development of software and the service provided to custodians of securities, we are the market leader with a 20% market share and nearly five million dollars in contracts.

We continue to support our employees in their career development. We are now at Grade C in skills acquisition, and soon, we plan to submit the file for the approval of our investment bank and an investment management company.

THE BRIGHT FUTURE

Through a strategy consulting firm with a Fintech orientation, we aim to:

1. Equip the actors of the sub-regional financial markets with the technological infrastructures required for the mobilization of mass savings, and the transparent and fluid management of large-scale financial market operations.
2. Popularize the law and practice of financial market operations.
3. Chart the path for business growth.
4. Promote companies' access to new financing sources.
5. Lead our customers' businesses to their digital age transformation.

Through the Mutual Fund, we are entering the field to change the rules of the game. With our first fund FCPI (Fonds Commun de Placement en Valeurs Immobilières), we aim to:

- Construct 10,000 housing units over the next 15 years.
- Change the way people invest in real estate in the sub-region and help to boost the sub-regional financial market as a REIT: Real Estate Investment Trust.

These activities correspond to the grade F and G in our employees career plan.

Through the brokerage company, we aim to build one of the best companies with high growth potential listed on the sub-regional stock exchange and to influence the thousands of companies with a management system focused on the development of human potential that has already proven itself.

PART II

WHAT DOES IT TAKE TO BECOME TRUSTWORTHY AND PROSPER?

Speaking of the natural increase in wealth, the Bible says in Luke Chapter 10, verse 16:

Good and faithful servant, you have shown yourself worthy of few things, greater things I will entrust to you, enter into the joy of your master.

So, the simple fact that you hold this book in your hand is not coincidence. You have reached the stage in your life where you have to say stop:

- STOP the denial of the fruit of fundamental values of work, trust, loyalty.
- STOP slander, defamation, aggression and blows against those who express themselves excellently in what they are good at.
- STOP to those who choose to bury their talent for fear of being rejected by their community.
- STOP to those who do not even dare to try because they have mastered the rosary of reasons why it will not work.

To become trustworthy and prosper, what does it take?

THE APOLOGY OF POVERTY

Any state of poverty is a deterioration of one's inner self because the self is in abundance. Below are some practical and ideological beliefs that fuel the state of poverty:

False beliefs: Poverty in all its forms has its superstructure of beliefs of which I will give you some characteristic elements:

- o **The denial of the fruit of fundamental values:** He who has money is necessarily a sorcerer or dishonest.

- o **The false humility:** In Africa, anyone who has talent in a particular field and who speaks about it with confidence and conviction in a state of mind of certainty is arrogant, full of himself. He must bring himself to the same level as the others to be considered modest and humble.

- o **The lack of faith:** the lack of faith justifies all the reasons why we cannot give our attention to all the possibilities available to us.

- o **A misperception of the purpose of life:** In our BAMILEKE culture, parents used to advise: grow, go to school, find work, get married and take care of your children. Such a way of thinking is difficult in an environment where workers are still paid on the basis of the civil servant code or collective agreements dating from the 1980s and where there have been two devaluations of the local currency and 800% inflation. In this context, how can you always have enough to take care of your family? In the human experience, everyone must find what excites him and must try to become the best version of himself.

○ **The lack of vision:** on our continent, many talents are buried because of the lack of vision. This phenomenon implies: the fact of doing little when you can do more for fear of hurting others, the fact of not sharing one's life experience with others for fear of being rejected, the fact that many people are unable to lead a high impact project over time. Each of us has a calling in a specific area where God expects us to take action to help him make the world a better place.

PART III

THE STRUCTURE ASPECT: A MINDSET THAT ALLOWS YOU TO BE TRUSTWORTHY

• **The importance of vision**
If your vision is great and if it serves to bequeath a better world to future generations, then the vision alone is enough to correct all the false beliefs that feed the state of mind of poverty.

• **The use of the only real resources that matter: free will and time**
You have to be careful about the causes you defend and the system of beliefs you choose to adopt, because your beliefs determine your values, define your choices, and maintain your dominant thoughts. Your dominant thoughts determine your actions and your actions lead to results and the sum of your results reflect your quality of life.

Be aware of your free will and practice it now to defend the right causes and support actions that provide solutions with the aim to improve life.

The second resource that counts is the use of time. How you exercise your power of free will determine how you use your time and indicate whether you can be poor or rich, sick or healthy, happy or unhappy.

To be trustworthy, integrate the importance of vision and make good use of only real resources that matter

- **Train to always surpass yourself:**
  If you are not progressing in your current situation, it simply means that you have to occupy more than your current area. The prosperity zone is beyond your current zone, and this may require some sacrifices.

- **The loyalty: unfailingly**
  Loyalty is the second capital in business. Your ability to keep your word is to do what you say. This builds your reputation and your reputation makes people believe in you for what you say, and the faith that people place in what you say gives you new opportunities and makes you prosperous.

A complicated situation is a privileged moment to know exactly what to do. It is an opportunity to return to the sources of life and to formulate the intention of what you need and entrust it to the Infinite Intelligence who renews the world every moment. And by keeping the faith, He who, every moment, renews the world will know how to guide us. William James says that the reservoir of divine providence is within us where we can draw on it to solve all our problems.

- **Be merciful to those entrusted to your care**
  In terms of shafting of approach, of collaboration and/or innovation in the way of transmitting knowledge in my career, the most important moments have been each time I had to deal with a mediocre student or collaborator. I usually wonder how I would like this guy to remember me: as the one who took away the possibility of a career in this company because I have fired him, or as the one who, despite his current incompetence, gave him both the time and the support necessary to adjust his skills and preserve his job and career. Then you know what my choice was.

- **Delay enjoyment**
  Any change in the standard of living requires a price to be paid. And you have to be able to find the necessary resources and to pay that price.

- **Be different and assume it**

  More than 98% of the world's population is made up of (1) the most disadvantaged social strata, (2) the intermediate social strata and (3) the middle class. They are real activists for equal opportunities and for gender equalities. But in my view, a good person needs to be part of the elite.

The elite influences politics and human organizations to reconfigure the world according to what seems good. The configuration of the world cannot lead to a healthy change by claims. The desired change will take place because more and more brave men and women have foreseen greater than working to bequeath an inheritance to their children. And thinking big nowadays is misunderstood, hated and isolated, but you have to accept the fact you are different from others, assume it, and stay focused on the impact your action will leave in your community, in your country, and in the world.

About Armand

Armand Djagueu founded Global Asset Cameroon in March 2020, as a fintech-focused strategy consulting company. Since then, Armand believes successful companies must combine digital using technological know-how. So his consultants therefore bring diversified sector and functional expertise to help executives better understand the challenges and opportunities associated with globalization. In just three years, his company has developed a software:

- to transform the way people invest in the regional capital market through the dematerialization of the securities transaction management system
- to improve the effectiveness and efficiency of traders' strategies in managing investment portfolios
- to accelerate the growth of people, teams and companies in any field of activity
- to guarantee the transmission of skills from present to future generations

Driven by his desire to support African capital market authorities with cutting-edge technological infrastructure through Morocco, Ivory Coast, Ghana, Zimbabwe, Botswana and Cameroon, Armand has now led 14 conferences for African capital market players over the past two years on integrated systems for managing dematerialized securities transactions. He has also been invited to explain the new regulatory framework for managing dematerialized securities transactions to legal professions, administrators and managers.

Today, his company has already helped to dematerialize and secure over $1 billion in assets and to guarantee the legal protection of the rights of some 6,000 shareholders.

In a sector previously occupied by multinational banks, Armand has built his brand on a management based on the development of human potential. Alone in March 2020, Armand has succeeded in training and retaining competent human resources through career paths ranging through grades A to F, and for which graduation from one grade to the next systematically involves the acquisition of new skills and the deployment of new activities. These are in the areas of expertise of software development companies, strategy consultancies, custodial and management account-keepers, merchant banks, coaching companies and the media.

Now, his staff is in Stage C, which marks the start of investment banking activities very soon. To go from where they are to where they want to be, they rely on their values (competence, loyalty, integrity), their missions, and the added value they create for their customers. They have the commitment of their whole team to a clearly-established vision and a concept of rewarding effort with fair and equitable remuneration.

Armand's ability to turn ideas into actions with high-impact results is such that a renowned editorialist in the media, who specialized in the practice of law and financial markets in Africa, has dubbed him **'the thinker who acts.'**

For its professionalism and internationally-recognized expertise, Armand's company was ranked the third best company in the top software development and top software testing companies in the USA in June 2023 by Design Rush.

Armand's company continues its adventure as a bridge between project promoters and financing solutions, with strong partners in Asia, Europe and even the USA, equipping capital market structures, custodians, management companies and central depositories with the appropriate software.

For any needs falling within the scope of the above expertise, please do not hesitate to contact Armand at:

- contact@globalassetcameroon.net

CHAPTER 9

SILENCING THE MIRROR

BY CHRISTINA ROBERSON-SMELTZER

Her finger pressed against the mirror, delicately tracing the contours of her youthful face. Her eyebrows were an unruly forest, one side reaching skyward while the other darted off in a sideways slant; metal braces equipped with rubber bands adorned her smile; her hair was an unruly mass of frizzy strands too wild for untrained hands to tame. As she stood, she assessed her outfit. It fit her well but just didn't look quite right.

Awkward and unsure in that moment of uncomfortable self-reflection she murmured, "This will have to do." Her big brown eyes welled up with the weight of unshed tears. Just before walking away from the mirror, her reflection whispered to her, 'You aren't beautiful.' As an unsparing critic, it berated her, 'You'll never fit in.' These taunts echoed back at her until finally, their voices faded into silence – leaving their mark on her young heart.

This little girl, still learning the meaning of self-confidence, had a tenacious spirit that refused to submit. Despite the societal pull of conformity, Christina refused to surrender to peer pressure as she set out on an epic journey towards self-discovery; finding her unique voice and accepting what God had designed just for her life, which, 'what-do-ya-know' was not the girl who fit in. That girl was Christina, version 1.0.

My childhood unfolded within the four walls of our home – an intimate classroom comprised of myself, my mom, my dad, and my younger brother. My parents implanted seeds of faith and morality deep within me—seeds I still treasure. The price for this secluded education, however, was my difficulty in carving a niche in the landscape of social norms. Little did I realize then, that the conformity I craved was a mirage best kept at arm's length!

The void of social interaction during my homeschooling echoed even louder when I transitioned to high school. Being engulfed in a sea of so many people was exhilarating, as it brought about the opposite sentiment of the loneliness I felt while homeschooled. However, in a crowd of 2,000+ teens navigating high school life, I often felt like just a number. I was still very much alone. Through those four challenging years, my true friends could be counted on one hand; this proved the truth of quality over quantity and I finally had the love and support I desired.

Embracing the minimal courage I could conjure up, I, the homeschooled geek, plunged headfirst into beauty school during my junior year. This leap of faith landed me a position in a high-end salon shortly after graduation. Here, amidst the swish of shears and hum of hair dryers, my confidence bloomed. It was a slow transformation. Despite shedding the physical tokens of my awkwardness—braces, headgear, and an untamed mane—it took me two years to feel at ease engaging my clientele beyond mere hair goals.

Those mirrors that used to reflect a timid girl now showed a woman budding with confidence. Yet, if I peered deep enough into my reflection, the phantom whispers of self-doubt would sometimes resurface. I could still hear the echoes of doubt that would taunt me all those years ago. 'You're still that same little girl,' the mirror bellowed. 'Your voice doesn't matter. You can't help anyone.' By this time, my resolve had hardened and there were no tears to be found. I had lingering uncertainty, but it was mixed with threads of hope.

I put my hands side-by-side and pressed my palms against the mirror's surface, blocking all but the outline of my face. With the slightest bit of confidence, I uttered to the mirror as I leaned in, voice shaking, "You're wrong!"

During my years behind the salon chair, I learned far more than the artistry of cosmetology. I discovered the joy and importance of forming substantial relationships—connections that held me when I stumbled and cheered when I triumphed. As these relationships grew stronger, so did my confidence. The mirror's insults faded into oblivion, replaced by the serene voice of God, guiding me, with peace and purpose.

After eleven years at the salon, I had not only made lifelong friends but realized that my true passion lay in not just making women look beautiful, but nurturing their entire beings. Their gratitude overflowed my cup with fulfillment and confirmed my divine calling.

In 2009, following a series of gentle nudges from a handful of clients, I dipped my toes into the ocean of the self-improvement world. After two years of researching and determining the best fit, I broke into the coaching industry in 2011, an instantly-fulfilling decision for me. A few years in, my confidence was soaring and I felt truly blessed to be living out my calling. Yet, I still struggled in my pursuit of 'success".

Once I moved my coaching to the online space, I began to understand what it felt like to share my message with an ever-expanding crowd. It was in those moments of feeling, once again, insignificant, that I also felt the most fulfilled. It was this odd combination of emotions that inspired me and proved most impactful. This culmination led to both my ability to relate to those who also felt small, inadequate, or alone, as well as the fulfillment that came with those invaluable connections.

When my words resonated with a lone soul or when shared perspectives helped someone overcome hardship, or even just being there when someone needed support during times of grief, were true moments of impact for me. Though my goals often felt insurmountable, like pedaling a stationary bike endlessly without progress, I began to relate to the thousands of bikers beside me who resonated with my same struggles. I found my deepest satisfaction in the simplest of moments.

My perception of success had completely shifted. I began to realize that the climb to success was not always upward. It also meant reaching deeper and allowing roots to take hold and spread. It is a vertical journey as much as a horizontal one. Success is about reaching out to those beside us, investing in them, growing with them, and supporting them.

A mantra echoed in my mind; an epiphany flooded my thoughts in an instant. I quickly and sloppily wrote it down on the first piece of paper I could grab...I read it...and re-read it again:

Turning the heads of thousands is not as powerful as touching the heart of one.

That message and those words have been engrained in my heart and forever will be. It now guides my path, reminding me of the true measure of my success. I have discovered the priceless reward of nurturing deep and meaningful relationships. Each heart that I touch, each life that I am privileged to impact, is an infinite treasure. The quality and depth of our relationships will determine the measure, impact, and reach of our success.

Success is not attained by following someone else's template for success, but by designing and implementing our own. Just as we add to or remove ingredients from a trusted recipe, there are some non-negotiable staples within the magic formula and some ingredients that are optional – based on our unique preferences. Just as there are steps in the cooking process, there are sequential steps in relationship-building as well.

Of the many ways we choose to navigate cultivating relationships as individuals, there are seven core elements we need to master:

1. Self-Awareness/Ownership and Responsibility

At the core of all effective relationship navigation lies self-awareness. By understanding ourselves, and our needs, and taking responsibility for our actions, we establish a solid foundation to navigate relationships effectively.

Before venturing into another's psyche, we must explore our blind spots and take ownership of areas of opportunity in our own lives. Only then can we make room to cultivate valuable relationships with others.

2. Alignment of Values

Aligned values are essentially the moral compass that guides our behaviors, decisions, and actions. When two individuals share similar values, they are more likely to respond similarly to life's events and challenges. In essence, trust and aligned values are the glue that holds relationships together. They provide relationships with the foundation to grow, thrive, and adapt in the face of life's unpredictability.

It's important to fully know ourselves in order to recognize what our value set is. Once we have a strong sense of self, the next pillar is trust.

3. Trust and Boundaries

Boundaries are the lines that define our individual comfort zones, and the limits to which we are willing to bend. After establishing a shared set of values, and a foundation of trust, setting boundaries, the next step, becomes natural; they're evidence of our faith in one another's respect – and so we put boundaries in place with the full assurance they will be respected by both parties involved.

We find the confidence to express ourselves openly about our comfort zones and the things we are not comfortable with. In this space of respect and understanding, a relationship can truly flourish.

4. Transparency and Communication

Transparency emerges after trust has been formed and boundaries have been put in place and upheld.

Trust propels us towards vulnerability, authenticity, and open dialogue. When we talk about vulnerability in relationships, we are referring to our ability to show our true selves to others, with all our strengths and flaws. Authenticity, on the other hand, is our commitment to staying true to our values, feelings, and beliefs, even when they may not align with those of others. The combination of vulnerability and authenticity births transparency, a state where honesty, openness, and clarity become the defining features of a relationship. By sharing our thoughts, feelings, and intentions, we strengthen connections and prevent misunderstandings.

This consistent communication is what helps facilitate and maintain that transparency.

5. Forgiveness and Healing

After establishing trust and transparency, a newfound comfort zone is created, a safe space where we can talk about our deepest fears, traumas, and past hurts.

These are issues that may have first come to light during the initial stage of self-reflection, the 'pillar one' of this transformative journey. Think of these issues as burdens we carry, invisible backpacks filled with guilt, shame, resentment, and anger. We have grown so used to their weight that we may not even realize how heavy they are until we decide to put them down.

Is guilt or shame keeping us tethered to the past? Is it making us revisit our failures and shortfalls repeatedly? Are we harboring resentment or anger, allowing them to poison our present and cloud our future?

The antidote lies in forgiveness. By mustering the courage to forgive ourselves and others, we carve out a space for healing and growth, not just within us but also in our relationships.

We cannot expect a wound to heal when shards of broken glass still plague the skin. It's the same as the emotional pain we endure from holding onto negative emotions. It's not until we recognize this, and consciously decide to remove these shards of anger, guilt, or shame, that the real process of healing can commence. However, it's vital to acknowledge that healing isn't a one-off event. It doesn't come with an expiration date.

There will be times when it seems easier to retreat into old patterns. It's during these times that we must be brave, lean on our foundations, and remember the peace that comes from forgiveness.

6. Vision and Plans

Healing is the gateway to the future. It's impossible to move into the future with one foot still planted in the past. It's comparable to being shackled, and those chains can be exceedingly hard to break.

When healing allows us permission to look forward to our future, we begin to see our vision. We are finally able to see clearly where we're heading. The past can, however, serve as a launchpad for our future, provided we learn from it and leave it where it belongs: behind us. Healing provides us with the key to unlocking these cuffs. No longer are we making decisions based on past pain, fear, or guilt, but instead, we make choices that align with our values, goals, and the person we aspire to become.

We begin to see how our relationships fit into this new, enlightened picture. We understand how these relationships either support or hinder our vision, making conscious decisions to nurture, realign, or, in some cases, distance ourselves from certain relationships.

Recognizing how these connections intertwine with our goals provides us the power to build stronger, healthier bonds.

7. Commitment and Action

This phase represents the point at which knowledge and understanding become the driving force behind our real-life choices and tangible action steps. It is where all the previous pillars combine and integrate into a lifestyle that upholds our values, goals, and vision for the future.

Commitment is about more than just a willingness to try and is not a one-time event. It is a promise to follow through. This level of dedication requires a certain degree of bravery. It's about remaining accountable; not just to those around us, but most importantly, to ourselves.

This journey towards commitment and action is not a comfortable one. It requires constant effort and discipline, consistently evaluating and reevaluating our actions. Here's the silver lining: the discomfort we feel is an indicator of growth. It signifies that we're stepping outside of our comfort zones, and we're curating new, healthier templates that uniquely fit us just right.

Commitment and action, then, are not just the conclusion but the continuation of our lifelong journey towards self-discovery, healing, and growth.

CONCLUSION

These seven pillars act as our compass, leading us through the complex maze of human connections. By embedding these pillars into our lives, we create a profound sense of accountability and mutual respect between ourselves and those whom we encounter here. As we transform through this process we leave behind imprints on the hearts we reach, touching lives in unimaginable ways. In turn, our lives are also forever changed.

Reflection

At one time, the mirror's criticism reverberated endlessly within my head. Through my journey, however, I realized that what needed silencing was my warped perception of self. My reflection was an array of insecurities, falsehoods, and confusion; an illusion in which faith was replaced with self-doubt while fear eroded confidence. That inner war had played out into physical reality.

Today as I peer into the mirror's depths, an astounding transformation awaits me. I no longer shrink away from my reflection. Instead, my head stands tall and my eyes meet its gaze directly. I realize that the mirror is no longer a mirror but an open portal; a window where my reflection has taken the form of a companion rather than an adversary. I now see resilience. I see love. I see grace. I see beauty. I see faith. I see purpose. I see connections.

I see me.

No longer does my reflection define me—my vision does.

I have silenced the mirror. Will you?

About Christina

With a heart devoted to serving others, Christina Roberson-Smeltzer thrives in roles where she is able to hold space, offer a listening ear, and provide accountability. Following lingering feelings of loneliness and the haunting reality of not fitting in during childhood, Christina's journey to adulthood began with a desire to improve and deepen the connections in her life. She pursued this goal both actively and subconsciously through multiple avenues.

During high school, she found an unexpected ally. Cosmetology became her chosen path, her outlet. Through her years in the Beauty industry she found a sense of community and discovered her own self-confidence, as well as how to inspire others to do the same. She developed a love for uplifting and supporting others, as she continued on her own journey of self-awareness and self-improvement. This eventually led to Christina becoming a Certified Professional Coach and founding her own coaching company and co-founding a nonprofit focused on Mental Health for youth.

As the founder of Discover A Better You, LLC and co-founder of Heart-Centered Matters, she focuses on building positive and lasting relationships, teaching essential life principles to people of all ages.

Christina, also known as 'The Coach Christina,' is an Entrepreneur who has been known to wear many hats, including Cosmetologist, Founder, CEO, Matchmaker, Coach, and Author. However, first and foremost, she is a mom and wife.

Christina's latest venture goes beyond her normal scope, expressing her values and beliefs through apparel. Her impactful line, Legacy Leaders, aims to raise awareness, empower others to find their voice, and advocate for causes they hold dear. Domestic Abuse Awareness, Equality, Empowerment, Mental Health Awareness, Giving Back and Anti-bullying are just a few causes Christina embraces and supports through Legacy Leaders.

Although her primary focuses are coaching and writing, wherever Christina's path takes her, you can be sure it involves enriching relationships, personal development, and heart-centered causes.

To keep up with Christina's present and future entrepreneurial adventures and get your fill of growth and connection, visit:

- TheCoachChristina.com

CHAPTER 10

MY SEDONA
SOUL ADVENTURE

HOW A BURNED-OUT DIVORCE LAWYER FOUND LOVE, HAPPINESS, PURPOSE AND A DIFFERENT KIND OF SUCCESS

BY DEBRA STANGL

From the outside, it looked like I had it all – successful attorney, married, living in a beautiful home that backed onto a forest, traveling to exotic places like Egypt. Coming from a background of private school and honors. My first job out of college was on Capitol Hill, as assistant to my Congressman, then as the assistant to former Supreme Court Justice, Abe Fortas, whose glowing letter of recommendation helped get me into law school. I established a private practice and was honored as the Chamber of Commerce's 'Outstanding Young Nebraskan' – it all looked good on paper.

What nobody could see was what I kept hidden – the alcoholic father, the enabling mother who withheld her love unless we were getting straight A's and excelling in everything we did (but who saved us from ruin when my father came very close to almost losing his business), the affair that went on for over 20 years (with my mother looking the other way and our 'family best friend' spending Christmas with us), the cervical cancer that started to eat away at my mother at age 47 (so obviously the result of the rage, frustration and 'stuckness' she was incapable of expressing) which eventually killed her 5 years later.

Whip that altogether and voila! You get a concoction culminating in a scared little girl (who felt and somehow 'knew' that something was 'wrong' but couldn't quite put her finger on what that something was). The scared little girl who became the scared big girl literally receiving her college degree in acting, then going out into the world 'acting as if' she was happy and okay. The truth was that she was a quivering mass of core wounds and insecurity, set up for the inevitable patterns – doomed relationships, unsatisfying, soul crushing (albeit lucrative) work, plus doing that work to exhaustion, and making a lot of money but never seeming to be being able to hold on to it and of course, the usual suspects of body issues (bulimia, constant yo-yo dieting and excessive, punishing exercise).

Fast forward 20 years to 1999: my parents' definition of success which has come (understandably) from their own wounds of being children of the Great Depression – 'If you work hard and make a lot of money, you'll be happy', 'Be more and do more so you can (ultimately) have more'– has manifested itself, resulting in me and my type A siblings (a doctor, a dentist, an engineer, and a financial consultant) all making a lot of money and all working much too hard.

We signed onto their definition of success. Were we happy? Not so much.

I was re-creating all my parents' patterns. The insanity that is the world of the adult child of an alcoholic has manifested in all the predictable patterns engendered in all that insecurity: I'm in yet another unhappy marriage (having provided the primary financial support, just like my mother had done), working too hard (just like both my parents did), $50,000 in debt (mimicking my parents' financial woes), weighing 40 pounds more than the actress body I had maintained in college (just like my parents' constant dieting), and the doctors having removed a lump which they've deemed not cancerous 'this time'. I'm 47, exactly the age my mother was when she got sick and died five years later. I'm unhappy, feeling stuck, hopeless, and frustrated (much like I remember my mother feeling).

But from the outside, it looked like I had it all.

It was the debt that haunted me the most, probably because my parent's (and society's) definition of success seemed to be so wrapped up around money. The debt had come from my (now) ex-husband's bad business decisions, but that didn't matter because we were married, so I was responsible. For five years, I would take on more cases, economize, etc., but nothing worked to reduce the debt.

During those five years, I would meditate and pray and say, "Dear God, I'm so unhappy, please tell me what to do." I had started on my spiritual path just after my mother's death years before and it had given me great comfort. At that time, I had discovered another world, I had discovered the connection with that highest part of myself, but now all these life circumstances had beat me down to the point where I couldn't seem to remember any of that anymore or take any comfort in it any longer. I was in total disconnection.

Amazingly, when I would ask God that question, oftentimes I would hear a very small voice that would say to me, "You need to leave your law practice." Whenever I would hear that voice, it would actually make me angry – "How can I possibly leave my law practice, I'm $50,000 in debt, nothing in savings, I'm our sole support, how can I possibly leave my law practice?"

The Universe was trying to show me the way. That Highest part of myself was connecting with me through my Intuition, giving me the exact information I needed for my highest good. And instead of listening, I was getting angry when I received the message.

I was doing weekly sessions with a therapist who was worried about me. She suggested a retreat. I suddenly heard the word 'Sedona' in my head. My Intuition was trying to blast through to me again.

Through a strange set of coincidences, I found Ranjita and her small retreat center above Sedona. When she asked if I wanted to do any sessions with her, I told her no because I really shouldn't have been spending the money on the retreat, much less doing sessions.

But as she and I sat in front of the crackling fire, I poured my heart out to her and she said something that shook me to my core: "Your law practice is sucking the life force out of you." Deep within, my Intuition whispered to let go of the money concerns and do the session

– a valuable nudge that changed everything. During that extraordinary experience, Isis, the winged Mother Goddess, enveloped me in her loving wings. She assured me that everything would be okay, but her words struck a chord, "If you don't leave your law practice now, you're going to die like your mother did."

They finally said it in a way I could hear it.

In a profound moment of realization, I saw my life paralleling my mother's story of sorrow, devastation, and sickness. Her unconscious choice became my conscious crossroads – did I want to live or follow her tragic path?

I yearned to live, but the thought of leaving my law practice seemed crazy. How could I walk away when we were $50,000 in debt, with no savings, and I was the sole provider? For two weeks after I got home, my lawyer brain spun in circles trying to figure out a solution.

Finally, in prayer and meditation, I reached out to the Divine, not begging or complaining, but simply seeking guidance. A profound energy surged through me, filling me with knowing and trust like never before. Gratitude washed over me, and I felt this amazing sense of surrender.

I was weeping as I got on my knees. "Okay, God, I get it that I have to do this and I'm going to do it. But you've got to give me some help here."

A few hours later an unexpected call from a former client reinforced my belief that I must listen to my inner knowing. He had purchased a new mortgage refinancing business and I asked him if it would be possible to refinance my house to get a lower monthly payment. Ten minutes later he called and said, "I can cut your mortgage payment in half, plus I can get you $50,000 in cash."

Because of my shame, I had never told him (or anyone else) that I was $50,000 in debt. Suddenly, in an instant, the weight of five years of worry and anguish was gone. The money piece – the definition of success I had always used – was handled.

It was handled within hours of asking God for help. It was handled within hours of going into that deep place of surrender and listening to my Intuition. I asked, I listened, I made a decision, and I got exactly the help I needed.

And that was just the beginning.

I spent the next three years going back and forth to Sedona for a month at a time to do deep healing work. I thought I would only be able to leave my practice for one year, but Tom's new internet marketing business bloomed, becoming an unexpected pillar of emotional and financial support, a gift for which I am eternally grateful.

Suddenly, in 2001, three weeks before 9/11, I was in Sedona doing a session in the same room where my High Self had appeared to me almost three years before. She appeared again as Isis, saying, "It's time to move to Sedona." I responded, "Why? What am I going to be doing in Sedona?" No response. One of the things I have learned over the years is that the High Self doesn't usually show you the complete picture, only the next step. Mine had shown me the next step.

My brain started kicking in, telling me how crazy it was to move to Sedona, it made absolutely no sense from a financial standpoint. But over those previous three years of doing all the work I had done on myself, the one thing I had definitely learned was how important it was for me to listen to my Intuition and do what I was being told.

Miraculously, within 24 hours, a newfound friend in Sedona extended an offer to rent her beautiful house while she journeyed through India. This unexpected kindness was another affirmation that following my Intuition was indeed the path of destiny.

The real estate agent said that it would take six months to sell the house; we sold it in three days for more than the asking price. Another sign that following my Intuition was the thing I had to do.

We moved to Sedona and I sat here for six months awaiting some insights, but nothing transpired. I would pray to God and say, "I did what you told me to do. I came here. Now what?"

Suddenly, over those next few months, I started having dreams about what would become my work, Sedona Soul Adventures. I knew from my own experience that the real transformations happened from me doing private, one-on-one sessions with these incredible Practitioners who are masters at moving and utilizing this energy, rather than group retreats or workshops.

I was being shown that I could condense the healing that had taken me three years into three or four days by using the same process – find, release and heal the core wounds, fears and limiting beliefs that are holding people back and then bring them back into connection with their Highest Self on all the levels – physical, mental, emotional and spiritual. And then, give them the tools and ongoing support to not only maintain this connection, but have it continue to grow and deepen. That became my vision and my mission as I embarked on the path to guide others in reclaiming their innate connection and living their fullest, most vibrant lives and finding and maintaining healthy, juicy, loving relationships.

That was over 20 years ago. Since then, we have helped tens of thousands of people with our private retreats which are custom designed for each individual or couple. Individuals leave happy, content, and at peace knowing their life's purpose and ready to live it. Couples are able to let go of the resentments of the past, rediscover the love that brought them together in the first place, and bring the sizzle back into their relationship. It's ironic to me that I was a divorce attorney for 20 years, and now I've spent another 20 years doing so much to save and renew countless marriages. Hopefully, the karma is balanced out by now! Even after all these years and helping thousands of people, I'm still amazed at what happens.

Over the years, I've had many people say to me, "Oh, you must have been so brave leaving your law practice. That must have taken so much courage." I never felt brave, I never felt like I was doing anything out of the ordinary. But when I look back on it now, I understand why people think that. I was not 'doing' success in the way most people do. I left the security of being an attorney, moved to another place and started a business with no capital and no guarantees, just listening to what I was being told **through my Intuition** and then doing what I was being told. It took me five years to finally start listening, but once I started listening, each next step just seemed like the logical thing to do.

As my healing journey continued, another lifelong issue was transformed—my body. From the tender age of three, I immersed myself in dance, which subjected me to constant scrutiny and body shaming. Endless dieting became the norm, and the cycle was all too familiar. Starvation and excessive exercise yielded temporary weight loss, but the moment I allowed myself to eat 'normal' food again, all the pounds (plus more) returned with a vengeance. My body became my enemy, and I yearned for a different way of being.

Using the transformative processes we teach here, a profound shift occurred. I immersed myself in a state of unconditional love for my body. Miraculously, I shed over 40 pounds without diet or exercise in under five weeks. It was a revelation! I now relish the freedom to eat and drink whatever I want, fully embracing my body and nourishing it with love and acceptance.

Yet, the greatest gift of all was finding my true soul partner, Richard. After 20 years together, Tom and I amicably parted and six years later I discovered I had a yearning to really experience a deep and profound love relationship and spiritual partnership. Through trusting my Intuition and utilizing the principles we teach here, I manifested the love of my life. Our connection was undeniable, transcending distance and expectations, leading us to marry amidst the red rocks of Sedona, surrounded by love and family and friends.

In a world fixated on prestige and financial success, I once embraced the beliefs of my parents and society. Looking back at the fascinating odyssey that my life has been, I realize the innate wisdom we all possess. It is within our power to seek, to listen, and to act on the whispers of our soul. The key to unlocking our true destiny lies in releasing the wounds and misperceptions of the past, connecting with that highest part of ourselves and trusting our Intuition, secure in the knowledge that it will guide us to the life we are destined to live.

Looking back today, I am so grateful for every step of this extraordinary journey – every challenge, every moment of surrender and every leap of faith. It has brought me a life where my work feeds my soul, abundance exceeds all my previous expectations, where love knows no boundaries, and where happiness surpasses imagination. My mission is to share these profound lessons and empower others to find their path to fulfillment and to live the lives they were meant to live.

So, dare to ask the Universe for guidance, open your heart to its whispers, and take inspired action. Success, when redefined through connection to 'All That Is', is the key to a life of peace, joy and bliss. Embrace the extraordinary journey that awaits and let your soul soar to new heights.

About Debra

Debra Stangl is an example of how life is full of second chances. In 1999, she was a divorce attorney in Omaha, Nebraska, hating her work, depressed, overweight and in an unhappy marriage. She came to the spiritual Mecca of Sedona, Arizona and had a spiritual re-awakening. Three years later, she founded Sedona Soul Adventures, which has a unique way of doing spiritual retreats. These are retreats for individuals and couples, not groups, and each 3-7 day retreat is custom designed for each person (or each couple) based on the Sedona Proven Process developed by Debra over 20 years ago, consisting of one-on-one or two-on-one sessions with over 60 of Sedona's Master Practitioners.

Sedona Soul Adventures has been featured on *The Today Show, USA Today, Forbes, The Washington Post, Yoga Journal* and *Elle*. They were named 'Best of Sedona' for Retreats in 2020, 2021 and 2022, 'Best Marriage Retreats' in the US (2017-2023) and 'Best Couples Retreats in the World' by *Brides Magazine* in 2022. They were named to the Inc. 5000 List of Fastest Growing Private Companies in the US in 2019 and again in 2023.

Debra is the author of the #1 International Bestseller, *The Journey To Happy – How Embracing The Concept That Nothing Is Wrong Can Transform Your Life.*

Debra also leads group trips each year to Peru and Egypt, allowing participants to connect with the energies of these sacred places.

Debra received her Bachelor's Degree in Theatre and Dance from the University of Iowa in 1974. After that, she lived in Washington, D.C. and was the personal assistant to Congressman Edward Mezvinsky, who was on the Judiciary Committee during the Watergate proceedings (and is now Chelsea Clinton's father-in-law). Next, she was the personal assistant to former Supreme Court Justice Abe Fortas who encouraged her to go to law school. Debra graduated from Creighton Law School in 1979 and practiced law in Omaha, Nebraska.

During that time, she was an advocate for women and children and wrote the Children's Trust Fund Act, legislation which funds programs for the prevention of child abuse. For her efforts, she was named one of ten 'Outstanding Young Omahans' in 1982 and the 'Outstanding Young Nebraskan' by the statewide Nebraska Chamber of Commerce in 1983. Debra practiced law for 20 years before her spiritual reawakening led her to leave her practice and ultimately relocate to Sedona.

Since founding Sedona Soul Adventures in 2002 and helping thousands of people transform their lives, Debra writes and speaks about how it is possible to live a life of joy and ease and purpose.

Debra lives in Sedona, Arizona with her husband and spiritual partner, Richard Kepple, and their two Doodles, Missy and Beauregard. Debra and Richard are currently co-authoring a book on relationships and for the past two years have been having a blast doing photo shoots for the book all over the world – in Paris, London, Egypt, New York, Chichen Itza, Stonehenge and, of course, Sedona…so far.

You can reach Debra at:

- Debra@SedonaSoulAdventures.com

Learn more at:

- http://SedonaSoulAdventures.com

CHAPTER 11

MY FIELD OF DREAMS HAD ROOTS IN NIGHTMARES

BY JUDITH A. HANCOX, MSW, LICSW

"If you do it, they will come."
"What about my insurance, pension plan, steady paycheck?"
"If you do it, they will come, and all will be taken care of."

It was 1997. My psychic friend Nancy was reminding me to trust my dream. I was a clinical social worker in a K-12 private school for special needs children—a caseload of over 60 by day, meeting with one or two clients in my home office at night.

School hours well exceeded contract hours. After years of positive evaluations, I asked for a raise and was told, "Salaries are set by the Board; we cannot pay what you deserve."

Although underpaid, I loved my job. I had a basket of requests at my door every day and I was helping students succeed. The thought of expanding my private practice was exciting, but I did not want to abandon the kids. I thought I would stay until retirement.

It reminded me of the time I thought I would never leave Vermont. What happened could be summarized by Carl Jung:

"There's no coming to consciousness without pain."

Bill and I met in 1970, the year I was gifted *Autobiography of a Yogi*. I had questioned, "Who am I? Why am I here?" since 8. At 18, I found reasons through the magic of love felt by soulmates. Created from love, for love, to give love to each other—our true sole purpose.

We were both affected by traumatic childhoods. Like the children I served, we each held subconscious negative self-beliefs that sabotaged our relationship with traumatic trajectories. It is no wonder I was led to a career in mental health and trauma recovery.

In 1973 we moved to the Northeast Kingdom of Vermont. Pregnant with new life growing within me and joy-filled hopes and dreams, we were excited, in love, thinking we would never leave the beauty of Groton State Forest. We swore we would never move back to New Jersey.

I grew lonely in the forest with our baby while he was out working. Missing contact with people, we moved near friends on the west coast of Vermont. It seemed a good fix.

Five years, three exhausting moves later, two unhappy people were packing again, hardly speaking. Anguished by a bankruptcy and broken dreams, we were moving back to New Jersey after all.

It took me years to realize my husband worked such long hours in his construction business to offer his family the love and support he had not received from his father. It took me years to understand I could not fill the trauma holes in my soul with anything other than my very own Self. It took us years to receive the therapies we needed to heal our childhood wounds.

> *Even in your greatest darkness, I am never separate from you.*
> ~Lord Krishna, Bhagavad Gita

Fall, 1978

One day, close to NJ moving day, I was feeling overall devastation. Hugging a tree on the bank of our beloved Lake Champlain, tears streaming down my face, I was a sobbing, blubbering mess. With fists held tight, I shouted to the sky: "Why is this happening!" Lost, confused, with insides shaking, I pleaded with an unknown entity, searching for a miracle.

"Please help me, take me, guide me! I can't do this on my own!" Repeating, "please!" and "help me" more times than I can count, I finally collapsed, exhausted. A feeling of warmth slowly stirred in my body. I trusted this feeling. I felt I was being listened to, and surrendered...surrendering brought peace.

I re-read *Autobiography of a Yogi*, the story of an Indian saint who experienced a life of miracles. Paramahansa Yogananda reassured me there is a higher power. I aspired to live a life of surrender as he did. It gave me back the hope I had tucked inside my heart eight years earlier. Yogananda's story enlightened me to the fact I had been living a life of Self-deception. Like a spiritual window shopper, looking briefly at many methods, I believed I could grow spiritually by reading books. I was a loving, caring mom and considered myself a spiritual aspirant, but I had been judgmental and insecure. Without the work of mastering our ego, it is difficult, if not impossible, to change deep-rooted traumatic imprints. Contemplation is important but does not transform behavior. I needed a living, authentic teacher.

The juxtaposition of moving North to VT and South to NJ seemed like our love compass turned upside down. We arrived with a caravan of friends in laughter and joy, and we left alone, weepy, and depressed.

Surrendering led me to unfamiliar territory. By trusting the process and saying "yes" to dauntingly different opportunities, doors opened. I was offered a government grant to attend Cook College to attain a license in environmental health and law—the last year a non-science major could take the course. I was given a scholarship to study Shiatsu (for skills I would need later to practice energy psychology).

We received financial assistance to purchase our first home in Stillwater—where I met my authentic "guru" teaching at the local library. After four years of yoga practice and studying the Bhagavad Gita with Swami Premananda, he proposed I renounce my worldly possessions and move into the monastery—if I was a serious spiritual aspirant.

I renounced. Bill and our son Jesse moved with me, though not so enthusiastically. I believed I had found my true purpose—to live there and teach yoga, forever. Two years later Swami disbanded the ashram, crushing my dream of living a monastic life. **I was shocked into submitting to the spiritual rip current pulling me in a different direction.** 1986 was the year I learned you can live and work anywhere as a renunciate by remaining non-attached to material possessions.

After working two years as health director for the Long Valley Health Department (appointed by the health officer who left on pregnancy leave and never returned), I asked for a raise commensurate with job responsibilities. The Board of Health said no, but they would fund my master's program in environmental science to become their official H.O.

I discovered a master's degree in social work administration allows one to take the Health Officer's exam. When permission to change to this desired program was denied, Bill and I paid for it.

Dr. Bernard Indik, my social work internship advisor, encouraged me to initiate Parents Anonymous in rural Sussex County where we lived. He had wanted someone to start this chapter for prevention of child abuse for years. He passed away two years after completing the mission, blessing me with the experience I needed to be hired by the special needs school I loved.

Its chief school administrator, my supervisor and awesomely creative psychologist, Dr. Jack Goralsky (Dr. G.) sent me to an EMDR (Eye Movement Desensitization and Reprocessing) training program in 1995. EMDR revolutionized our therapy sessions with students. The primary treatment was cognitive behavioral therapy (CBT), with rewards and consequences for behavior. EMDR facilitates bilateral brain stimulation to access the root of a problem and *change* behavior.

One student was school phobic and permitted to go directly to my office every morning, usually in tears. After unproductive weeks with CBT, our first EMDR session desensitized the trauma causing his fear. After two sessions his phobia was extinguished, along with morning visits.

Albert Einstein said miracles are simply undiscovered science; this science-based therapy was simply miraculous! It was an exciting time to be at this school and I looked forward to each day. Outside school, I was a board member of the Holistic Alliance International, sponsoring annual health fairs and learning alternative, complementary healing modalities from keynote speakers—renowned leaders in their field.

Realizing less was more when it came to medicating students, most of our students were over-medicated. I was the sole faculty member advocating non-pharmaceutical means of treatment. After referring a parent to a specialist in Neural Organization Technique (N.O.T.), her daughter ran into my office a few weeks later, holding her first 100% on a spelling test! This dyslexic student had failed every spelling test to date and struggled with low self-esteem. Now she was jumping in joy, proclaiming, *"Mrs.H! I could see the words on the page spelled right for the first time!"* The treatment changed her life—and mine.

When the administration asked if I was getting 'kick-backs' from doctors for my referrals, I was mortified. It was like a splash of ice water on my psyche—a wake-up call. I felt like shouting, "Are you crazy? I'm a renunciate; it's not about money!" I felt disappointed, frustrated, sick to my stomach.

My present self would tell my younger self, "Feelings are your guidance system saying something is wrong. Your ego wants to argue and create friction. You need to be silent, listen to your intuition." I thought I could change the system, but not without the blessing of the people who created it.

My psychic friend Nancy was right. I took the leap of faith that year and my private practice was thriving within six months. Bill created my slogan, *'Therapy Doesn't Have to Last a Lifetime!'* witnessing the accelerated pace of people healing from trauma. With a population of over five million people, New Jersey seemed to be the place I needed to be!

1999 was a year of profound change. I co-produced my first guided meditation with *Angelic Sea*—a musical composition with auditory bi-lateral brain stimulation for EMDR. The composer claimed, "I received this music from the angels."

The EMDR International Association accepted my proposal to present *'Transformation of Energy in EMDR'* at their 1999 conference. I asked my friend, psychic medium Nancy O. Weber, R.N., to co-facilitate. Nancy holds an honorary detective badge in NJ and is a brilliant facilitator with unique insight.

1999 was also the year I met Shiome, my Maui 'power animal' who guided me in circles under the sea. I was twice blessed with this wild dolphin entrainment when she *visited me* months later in a personal EMDR session, telling me her name, and how to spell it! Researching 'Shiome,' I found it means *'rip current!'* (*Something Special*, Shiome. com.)

In the rip current of my professional life, I learned from many masters. Grandma Mechi Garza, Cherokee Medicine Woman and Shiome taught me how to transform energy in a 'medicine wheel,' or 'magic circle,' fundamentally changing darkness to light. Creating *Shiome Therapy* was essential for these current times, where I have been pulled into deeper and darker waters.

On September 11, 2001, our town lost many residents working at the twin towers. I volunteered my service for survivors. One client could not get a disturbing picture out of his mind. His fiancé, a soul who was on the plane that crashed into a tower, gave him a message in our EMDR session.

She told him, "Everyone left the plane before it hit the tower. Our angels escorted everyone off the plane. No one suffered physically." That message brought peace to my traumatized client, and to me. Research has documented numerous cases of messages received from departed loved ones during EMDR sessions. I now teach one modified method, *Repair and Reattachment Grief Therapy* (repairandreattachment.com).

Being guided to faster and faster methods of trauma recovery is a double edge sword—taking me to the deepest depths of human suffering, as well as the highest heights of spiritual healing.

I learned about high grade essential oils that raise energy frequencies. I learned *Evolving Thought Field Therapy* which guided me to create an *Energy Correcting Meditation*—moving meridians, vessels, and chakras from negatively stuck in reverse, to positively flowing forward, within seconds, guaranteeing peaceful meditations. Recently, I learned the *Flash Technique* (Dr. Philip Manfield) which assists facilitating trauma recovery with large groups.

Dr. G. once laughed, *"Shiome Therapy* is like my grandma's chicken soup recipe—a little of this and a little of that."* Yes, *Shiome Therapy* is my chicken soup for the traumatized soul. And in 2013, I became part of a group with thousands of traumatized members.

I will never forget my sister's horrified expression after receiving her daughter's diagnosis: 'Stage 4, esophageal cancer.' We were in the hospital hallway when she shook her fist and cried, *"God would not take my only child!"* It was two days before Carly Elizabeth Hughes' 24th birthday. She left us four months later.

Racing down Route 80, we received the call: *"You do not have to rush, she just passed away."* Stunned, I mumbled repeatedly, "She's not dead, she's not dead, she's not dead…" while Bill drove in tears; we arrived at the hospital in silence. What could I say to my sister? I needed to assure her Carly was OK.

My godchild assured us within days. She 'visited' my friend Nancy, specifically directing us to create *'Carly's Kids Foundation for Education,'* for the needy children she had volunteered for on earth. Carly gave me messages in dream visits and on my cell phone!

My sister, Irene Vouvalides, was guided to Helping Parents Heal (HPH) for support. She is now vice president. HelpingParentsHeal.org— with 25,000+ members and growing—was co-founded by Elizabeth Boisson and Mark Ireland to help bereaved parents become 'shining light parents'—shining their child's light of love on humanity.

I learned through Irene that most bereaved parents unknowingly suffer with post-traumatic stress disorder (PTSD). Through evidential science and spiritual guidance, I can now gather groups of HPH parents remotely, helping them heal from their traumatic stress.

The world is only in the mind of its maker.
~ A Course in Miracles

Once, during a school-rewards trip, we took students to play miniature golf. At the last hole a teacher remarked, "You won't make this one, *I know this hole is impossible.*" I looked at my student and said, "Just focus on the hole and putt it in." She made the hole in one. Turning to the teacher I advised, "Never tell them anything is impossible."

Anything is possible when you are in alignment with your true Self. It is a matter of trust.

Nightmares are power dreams—messages from our higher power. The mantra, *'Only Love is Real,'* helps awaken us from our sleep, reminding us who we are, and how to manifest beautiful dreams.

I am writing to you from our dream home in Vermont, back on our beloved Lake Champlain. We have returned, full circle—wiser, more compassionate, non-judgemental, and forgiving. We know world peace begins with inner peace, and we focus on that task each day.

Through our worst nightmares, Bill and I have kept our eye on the goal—trusting each other's soul.

We know, when sowed with love,
all is taken care of in your field of dreams.

About Judith

Judith A Hancox, MSW, LICSW, BCETS, Founder of Shiome Therapy, is a clinical social worker specializing in holistic trauma recovery. Certified in yoga, meditation, and philosophy, she received her B.A. at William Paterson University, and MSW at Rutgers University. She is a member of NASW, EMDRIA and AAETS.

Judith is an EMDR-Certified Therapist, certified in Flash Technique, Gestalt Therapy, Evolving Thought Field Therapy, Repair & Reattachment Grief Therapy (RRGT), and Past Life Regression Therapy, trained by Dr. Brian Weiss. She is licensed in New Jersey, Vermont, and certified for telehealth in Florida.

Facilitator of *Shiome Therapy*™, Judith guides trauma survivors to their highest potential of emotional recovery and strength of spirit. Shiome Therapy is a synergistic interweave of evidenced-based psychotherapeutic modalities and creative, indigenous protocols developed for individuals and groups. She facilitates certification training for individual and group *Shiome Therapy*, and for *Repair and Reattachment Grief Therapy.*

Judith founded Parents Anonymous of Sussex County, NJ, in 1988. In the 1990's Judith was a member of New Jersey Assemblyman Catania's Professional Roundtable for Prevention of Child Abuse, served as program coordinator for DASI, Sussex County's Battered Women's Shelter, and worked as a public and private school child study team member and clinical social worker. She was a frequent guest on 'Body, Mind, Spirit,' a Morris County, NJ Cable-TV series, and guest panelist on Channel 9 WWOR-TV's 'NJ Matters.'

Co-creator of *Mirror Image Workshops for Self Esteem* with Nancy O. Weber, endorsed by the New Jersey Education Association for its presentation at NJEA's Atlantic City Convention, Judith facilitates professional workshops nationally and volunteers for non-profit organizations, most recently, Helping Parents Heal (HPH), as an HPH Caring Listener, and facilitating monthly *Shiome Healing Circles* for HPH members.

Judith presented *'Helping Parents Heal PTSD,'* at HPH's Conference in Phoenix, AZ (2018), at Desirae's Gathering at the Omega Institute, Reinbeck, N.Y. (2019), and for HPH's International Conference in Phoenix, AZ, August 2024.

Creating Healthy Boundaries (1999) is her guided visualization with *Angelic Sea,* a musical track with auditory bilateral brain stimulation and ocean sounds, by composer Munro DeJohn. It can be implemented for EMDR, meditation, concentration, and enhanced relaxation.

Judith's book and CD/digital recording, the *Energy Correcting Meditation,* (ECM, latest edition 2022) is essential for people searching for inner peace. It offers a six-minute and sixteen-minute meditation with six pressure points that move the body's energy systems in a positive direction, efficiently and expediently, offering choices of positive affirmations related to each point. The book gives essential information for healing the body, mind, and spirit.

Her upcoming book, *Transforming Nightmares to Nirvana: Shiome, the Way, (Introducing Shiome Therapy - A Body, Mind, Spirit Approach to Accelerating Trauma Recovery!)* will be available soon!

Judith lives in Vermont with her husband, Bill, and their pets, Apache and Shanti. She enjoys reading, writing, gardening, cooking, swimming, boating, and learning to sail on Lake Champlain.

Learn more at:

- shiome.com
- judithhancox.com
- whitewolfcenter.net

CHAPTER 12

HOW I FIRED MY MOM!

BY PA ANN SOMMER

You fired your mom? Yes. I did, and this is why.

THE SHY ONE

Have you heard the song lyrics: "One of these things is not like the others, one of these things doesn't belong..." It was on a TV show called *Sesame Street*. Well, I was that 'one thing'...meaning my four siblings were all brunette, confident, verbal, and fearless.

And then there was me, 'Ann'. I was the only sibling with naturally blond and curly hair, shy, and scared of everything: dogs, dark, lightening, thunder, heights, people, talking and strangers. I would blush at everything, especially if my name was called out loud in a crowd or school. My face would feel warm, then hot, like a quick flame on a stove top to boil water. And that was the next sensation, like boiling water, my face would turn RED HOT and it burned from my forehead to ears to chin. This physical travesty alone was embarrassing but there was always that one person that had to exclaim, even louder than my name being said, with the added statement of: "Your face is turning so red!!!" In my head I was screaming, "SHUT UP!" After the obvious was pointed out, and everyone that didn't see me turned their necks like owls – 180 degrees around – to peer at my octopus-like color change. Well, that just made things worse because my face became burning hot and turned a cinder red. After the color faded back to baseline, my skin felt like it glowed for hours. It was horrible.

Regarding that 'one kid' that always had to be the 'hero' and point out my 'red face'. I just want to claim gratitude that I was shy and quiet, because the adult me visualizes a very different action and reaction toward the mouth of the person that always had to point out this very obvious facial anomaly. I envision a style of 'Allie McBeal' show, where she gets mad and turns into a lion and attacks the irritant.

The act of my Facial Blushing was out of my control, there was nothing I could do to avoid it. I tried holding my breath, breathing air up onto my face like a cool breeze, using paper as a fan, and the list goes on. Eventually I did find that magic cure: AVOIDANCE. I avoided any awkward encounter by standing far, far away, from the teacher or center of attention. From elementary through high school, I couldn't break the horrific red face. Internally, I so desperately wanted to raise my hand and answer in class, talk to new kids, and sing with my cousins as we recorded a song on the tape recorder, but I just couldn't.

MOM & DAD

When my parents got married, they ran a large dairy farm in the Midwest, and had five kids in eight years, I was number four of those five. Growing up on a farm that milked cows, raised calves into grown cattle, planted fields of crops, harvested those crops, cut hayfields and then turned that hay into bails, plus the house chores and the lawn chores, the 'sin' of sitting down... Just know we were always busy, because if there was down time and mom saw us being 'inactive', the statement was: "Find something to do, it's a sin to waste a beautiful day." And if we didn't find that something, mom would assign a 'something' that wouldn't be fun. I want to note there was no sleeping in on weekends, moms tag line was, "Get out of bed, people die in bed." She always made her message and end goal clear.

We worked as hard as my parent's, milking cows, shoveling cow poop, bailing hay on the hottest days of summer, and picking rocks out of the crop fields to avoid machinery damage during planting. My parents demanded perfection in work and self-expectations, but they led the pack and worked by our sides. I grew up understanding the value of a penny, a sweat bead, siblings as playmates and the enemy. Most days were survival of the fittest, with freedom to roam among the farm, fields, and woods for hours…to reappear in early evening to mom's comment, "Where did you all go?", which means she did not know we were missing for hours until her eyes saw our dirty faces reappear. This freedom and the 'find something to do' instruction, taught us independence, how to play, run, hide, and get lost in a forest – but also how to get back home. (The secret to getting lost in wooded areas is find the outside border of the woods, walk the outer perimeter until you can visualize Your house…may take hours but guaranteed you'll get home, combat anxiety, and learn some cool 'survivor' tricks.)

Mom & Dad: They were married almost 60 years before dad died at almost 85. They were German, so love was shared with a nice warm home, clothes, and homemade meals always eaten as a family. There was no, "I love you, great job, you're awesome, no hugs, no kisses… Never." Dad showed love with work, teaching, yelling and bad instructions, as we learned how to start and finish large farm jobs. When I was around age 10, up on a huge John Deere farm tractor (because only John Deere was worthy), the tractor engine was always running and very, very loud. His instructions to us went like this: he would start rambling words off, or instructions, about how to drive and operate the mechanics of this tractor. At the same time, he would fly his right hand rapidly in movements that meant something very clear to him. His large hand would go from one lever to the foot pedal to "don't do this" and then he was gone! This is how dad gave us major instructions throughout out childhood! What we learned quickly was the act of asking more questions – which meant don't ask because the instructions did not change or elaborate except with an ending from dad of "got it?" and then he was again gone. My little head learned the reply: "Okay, figure it out, don't mess up and use your commonsense God gave you. And by 'mess up' I mean do not F*BEEP* UP."

Mom was sweet and salty. In addition to working the farm with dad, she cooked, baked, canned everything for winter, decorated, sewed, led groups of kids in 4-H and our family. Her biggest gift to me was teaching me to sew; she was patient, clear and I loved everything about our time and sewing. I loved listening to how material has a grain, how to fold it, pin patterns correctly, and cut and follow the directions to meticulously construct articles of clothing or accessories. Me and sewing bonded! As I aged and mastered sewing, I was able to go solo, review a pattern, the instructions and figure out shortcuts of efficiency.

This was my outgoing personality soaring in a quiet setting.

<u>ADVICE: DAD</u> – He gave me advice in a yes or no format. He listened to my question, and answered in a way that led me to a swift conclusion.

<u>ADVICE: MOM</u> – She gave me a lot of words that felt like I was in a cyclone sentence, grasping for a period and a conclusion which I never seemed to get. We spoke different languages but used the same words.

HIGH SCHOOL

By my junior year in high school, about age 16-17, I mastered the skill of sewing and decided to make my own Junior Prom dress. We had a material store in town that had the best 'scrap table', we always found beautiful pieces for affordable prices, and that is exactly what I found for my dream dress. The material was a blue satin, but the Royal blue that is always pretty in all different lights and a lace that glistened like peacock feathers in the bright sunshine, to say it was beautiful is an insult. It was extraordinary. But there was a problem, the scrap pieces were smaller than the dress pattern recommended. I bought them anyway.

Once I was alone and cut out all the pattern pieces that I needed to pin onto the material, and then cut out the material perfectly as outlined by the pattern, I'd be in business. Because I had to do some creative cutting to use every millimeter of material, my head had reviewed the pattern and the instructions before I cut anything. At this point I was able to methodically read the instructions and figure out how to combine steps for efficiency and better construction. By the time I had every piece cut to begin construction of the prom dress, I had every step memorized in my head.

The day I chose to sew the dress together I was alone in the downstairs sewing room, door closed, just me, my instructions, the sewing machines and my quiet heaven. This was no small task, but I loved every step of the process, and I was content doing it solo, and all day long... I left my sewing room to empty my bladder only!

In late afternoon, mom knocked on the door, she opened it to check on my progress, I explained my steps to her and felt pride with her expression of being impressed. When I finished telling her the plan, she started to tell me about a step that wouldn't work, why it wouldn't work, how I had miscalculated the plan and made a recommendation. As I followed her recommendation and sewed two pieces together, then moved onto the next step of my plan, I was shaken to the core with this fact: Mom was wrong.

Well, to undo a seam in satin material is not a small task because I painstakingly removed each stitch, one by one, holding my breath to not pull too hard and run a seam out of the main pattern piece. As I sat there with the seam ripper, undoing what I knew was wrong, I became mad, and with each stitch, I became madder and madder and madder, and eventually my anger burst open my lips, and my tongue lashed out all over my mom. I do not recall exactly what I said, but it was a basic, "Get out, I don't need you misleading me anymore, I got this!"

After she left, I sat there steaming...I was so mad at her, and I was so much madder at myself. I knew she was just trying to help, but again her advice always felt like that windstorm of where's the period and conclusion, and I was usually misled as we did not have a great way of conversing with a goal of getting to an equitable conclusion. Every cell in my body chanted, "I knew what I was doing, why did I let her mislead me, I KNEW my steps were right, why did I listen because I KNOW I HAD EVERY STEP RIGHT!"

The next step in my prom dress and life were drawn from my next thought: "I am firing mom's advice in my life. I always know the right answer in my gut, but so desperately want her input, and when I follow it, I get led down a wrong road, then I am mad." I knew right then and there, I did not need her input, advice or blessing because she had taught me everything I needed to know about finding direction, analyzing patterns, people, environments and adjusting the steps that suited me best. Both my parents gave me trust to take a large-scale farm project and get it done right, they allowed me to play with my siblings in the snow making forts, sliding down the barn roof into the huge snow piles, run barefoot across the lawn, bike all over playing 'cops and robbers', chore responsibilities, and at night running warm water for baths with clean jammies and sheets to be tucked in nightly by them both.

After this self-declaration, I decided that being shy was hard, I was sick of it, and I was going to figure out how to become 'unshy'. I formulated a plan to observe, watch and memorize what other people did when they interacted. I watched body language, facial expressions, vocal tones, and every little detail...I would take in slowly. I would practice and mimic things until I felt brave enough to put my new lesson into practice. Sometimes my learned skills went well, sometimes they didn't. One day, in high school, I was talking to a male friend, and he said something funny...so, I laughed, I laughed so cute with a sweet little expression. So, imagine my shock when the reply back to me was: "Don't get mad Ann, geez!"...WAIT! LESSON TIME, ANN... apparently what I was showing in expression and body language was NOT what was being perceived by my talking opponent. Next step, figure out what certain facial expressions feel like...use a mirror. I then started to smile and then hold that expression and then look into the mirror. There were many 'AHHA' moments. My training continued for a long, long time and continues up to today.

I am happy to report that I not only figured out how to grow out of 'blushing', but out of Shyness as well. I have overcorrected and am genuinely happy, confident, outgoing, well-adjusted and still know when my path is correct.

Regarding mom...

Yes, I fired my mom that day, and I never rehired her. I didn't have to because I had turned into her.

[LIFE LESSON: Be open to learn everything that makes you happy, these lessons teach you self-trust and this will lead you into the greatness of you becoming you.]

About Ann

PA Ann Sommer is a Physician Assistant Medical Provider, author, speaker, consultant/coach, and thought leader. She is known for 'L.A.F.', which is both her logo and philosophy: Love, Acceptance and Forgiveness. She is a Truth and Change Expert: building lives with clarity, direction, and legacy. She transformed her own life from being shy and reserved to outgoing and confident. Ann's experiences have led her to become a leader, speaker, coach, and motivator. She has worked in various medical fields, including general medicine, vascular surgery, orthopedics, gastroenterology, women's health, and obstetrics/gynecology.

Ann's mission is to lead people towards positive change, helping them find laughter, excellence, freedom, and create a self-legacy. She believes that every person shares the truths of being born and eventually passing away, and she emphasizes the importance of living a fulfilling life and leaving behind a meaningful legacy.

Ann's magnetic personality and sense of humor have earned her praise from renowned individuals like Jack Canfield, author of *The Success Principles* and *Chicken Soup for the Soul*®. She is described as vibrant and often leaves people wondering what she will say or do next. Ann received her education from King's College Physician Assistant Program, Yale School of Medicine, Norwalk Hospital Surgical Residency, and A.T. Still University, where she earned a master's degree in PA Studies and Sports Medicine.

You can connect with PA Ann Sommer through her website: www.paannsommer.com, where you can find her contact information and learn more about her work. She is also active on YouTube and Facebook.

CHAPTER 13

THE DEMISE OF THE WARRIOR WITHIN

BY STACEY PITCHER

When I was a child, I adapted habits to survive and develop coping mechanisms to deal with emotional and dramatic events. Without even realizing it, I built walls and become more and more reserved, sometimes appearing cold-hearted. At the tender age of six, I witnessed a trauma in my home – my father pushing my mother against the wall as she bit him on his hand, and he let her go. My mother took me, my sister, and my brother into the car. I remember looking out the back window as we drove away from the house. It was just like a scene from a movie. Little did I know that this moment would mark the end of my life in that house, as my parents eventually got divorced. I understood that my story was not unique. All of us have a journey and that journey has pain in one form or another.

As we grow older, we often become defined by our pain, and it becomes the lens through which we see the world. How people have hurt us and done us wrong. This allows our joys and happiness to be taken away because we are hyper-focused on the negative things that has happened to us. We build these walls to protect ourselves from ever feeling that type of pain again, a coping mechanism we developed as children when we couldn't handle such emotional burden. However, as adults, we have the capacity to confront these painful experiences and grow from them.

Unfortunately, I was so gripped by fear and pain that I spiraled into depression and self-hatred. At the age of 16, I even attempted suicide, but my family's reaction was far from supportive. They dismissed my struggles, calling me stupid and selfish, brushing off my pain as insignificant. Well, the next year my life would truly test me to see if I wanted to be alive. Life is funny in the way that on the surface you can seem like you have it all together and you are super successful, but truly, inside you are falling apart. Let me show you what I mean.

During my final year of high school, I achieved several significant accomplishments. I held the title of Miss Teen Bermuda, an incredible opportunity. Additionally, I was elected as Student Council President and Yellow House Captain. Throughout the year, I actively participated in football, basketball, and the glee club, and we proudly won the football championship. Alongside these achievements, I played a role in building our yearbook and maintained an above-90 average in all subjects except Literature.

However, amidst all these successes, life presented me with challenging circumstances. In November, my mother was diagnosed with breast cancer, and a month later, my father was diagnosed with stomach cancer. This wasn't my first encounter with cancer, as I had previously lost my beloved uncle and aunt to the disease when I was younger. Despite these difficult moments, I recognized the strength and resilience within me.

On the day of graduation, I was honored with the Leadership award and the Outstanding Student Award, making it seem like I embodied the definition of success. But deep down, I learned a valuable lesson about pushing myself too hard. After graduation, I accompanied my mom to Boston for her radiation treatments, and during that time, I visited three different doctors for my own health issues. It turned out that I had shingles at the age of 18, a condition usually seen in seniors, not high school students. The doctors attributed this to extreme stress, which had taken a toll on my body.

This experience made me realize that true success isn't just about accomplishments and titles; it's about maintaining balance and well-being. Fortunately, both of my parents recovered from cancer, but it was a reminder that life's journey is more than just a list of achievements. We all have our unique stories to share, and this is mine—a tale of resilience, growth, and the importance of caring for oneself.

Fast forward four years, and I find myself in my final year of university, having been elected as the Vice President of Finance. During this time, my mother's cancer returned, and she fought bravely for a year. She witnessed my graduation ceremony, but tragically, just 13 days later, she passed away. The pain and sense of abandonment I experienced were indescribable, and it left me feeling completely numb.

In that state of numbness, I unintentionally hurt others. As the famous saying goes, *'hurt people hurt people.'* It took me a while to understand this, but I now recognize how blinded I was by my own pain, unable to see the pain I inflicted on others. I deeply regret the hurt I caused, and it's only now, at this point in my life, that I can truly acknowledge it.

To cope with the vast emptiness within me, I sought distractions in relationships that weren't fulfilling and turned to substances. None of these attempts helped, and in my destructive state, I turned to religion as a sort of band-aid for all the suppressed pain and hurt in my life. I was expecting a quick fix from a higher power without taking responsibility for my own actions or facing my deep-rooted issues. Only last year did I start to confront myself honestly and look inward.

It was a profound moment when I realized that the root problem was my lack of self-love. I found myself engaging in negative self-talk, doubting my intelligence despite being a CPA with an MBA, questioning my appearance despite winning a beauty contest, and doubting if anyone could truly love the real me, despite having amazing friends. I learned that I didn't need external validations to feel worthy, but my shadows were trying to convince me otherwise. Instead of running away in shame, I chose to embrace all aspects of myself—the good, the bad, and the ugly. By facing my shadows, I came to understand that I was the one blocking my own light.

In my past, I used to take great pride in being a warrior, someone tough and even harboring a hint of violence. In my mind's eye, I'd envision myself as a formidable princess, adorned with a crown on my head and a shotgun in hand, believing that this portrayal exuded a sense of badassery. Little did I know that this mentality was nothing but a fortress, a protective shell erected around my heart, obscuring my true self from the world. This persona was merely a response to the traumatic experiences I had endured, molding me into a materialistic individual, unable to form deep and meaningful connections with others. Regrettably, I allowed myself to walk away from lifetime friends without a second thought. I am not proud of these actions or choices, but I take full ownership of them, as they have served as powerful life lessons.

This warrior persona, it was nothing more than a survival mechanism I had adopted. My belief that the world was out to get me, constantly pushing me to protect myself at all costs, fueled this facade. Looking back now, I ask myself if I ever truly needed to face the battles alone or if my refusal to let others in was the true cause of my isolation. Self-sabotage was a recurring theme in my life, especially when it came to romantic relationships. I readily blamed my family history and past traumas for this pattern, failing to recognize that my perfectionism was a direct response to those internalized feelings of shame and inadequacy.

Over time, I have come to understand that perfectionism is a trauma response—a way to cope with the deep-seated shame and perceived defectiveness within myself. The constant pursuit of flawlessness became an exhausting endeavor, hindering my progress and keeping me stuck in a perpetual state of waiting. I would wait for the ideal partner, the perfect circumstances, or until I had everything meticulously planned out in my mind. This approach only resulted in stagnation, preventing me from moving forward in life. I have learned that is it better to get things done than for things to be perfect.

Playing the victim was another inclination that held me back. For far too long, I felt as though my life was at the mercy of external forces, attributing my struggles and setbacks to others. It wasn't until a pivotal moment when I found myself crying, my emotions laid bare, that I realized the profound truth—I had allowed pain and fear to govern my life. Taking inspiration from Jack Canfield, who emphasizes taking 100% responsibility for one's life, I understood that I am not defined by my decisions, and I always possess the power to change. It takes a true warrior to heal and feel the pain of their traumas and take responsibility for the actions.

This journey of healing and self-discovery has opened my eyes to the necessity of embracing all aspects of myself—the beautiful and the ugly. We each hold both light and darkness within us, and it's essential to recognize that neglecting the light will only allow darkness to prevail. I had grown accustomed to presenting a hard, cold, and strong exterior, believing that it was the only way to survive. However, to transition from mere survival to a life of flourishing, I must let go of the perception that the world is a battlefield against me. Instead, I've come to realize that the world is encouraging me to embrace my true self and radiate my light—something the world desperately needs.

The demise of the warrior lies in dismantling the walls that once made my world feel cold and lonely. It involved recognizing that true strength comes not from building barriers, but from tearing them down to embrace vulnerability and forge authentic connections with others. It is essential to realize that shedding the warrior veneer doesn't mean discarding the qualities that defined it. Instead, it means adopting those attributes in a different light – using courage, resilience, and determination to build bridges of understanding and compassion. The warrior within can still be harnessed for positive endeavors, advocating for justice, and protecting what is dear, all while promoting love and harmony. In this transformation, the warrior becomes a beacon of hope and support, cultivating a life of purpose and genuine human connection. This is an area that I am still learning and growing with every new experience and encounter in life.

Living in the safety of my comfort zone had its appeal, but I now understand that true growth and joy lie in stepping beyond those boundaries. Confronting my fears, acknowledging my vulnerabilities, and being authentic are all pivotal to my journey towards self-empowerment and happiness. Each step I take towards embracing vulnerability brings me closer to the true success I can attain in life.

My past experiences as a warrior have been essential in shaping who I am today. However, I now comprehend that this persona was simply a coping mechanism—a protective barrier around my heart. I've learned refining the warrior within and embrace vulnerability, for it is on the other side of vulnerability that I find true success and happiness. Embracing my entire self—the light and the darkness—allows me to thrive rather than merely survive, and it is this growth that brings a newfound sense of joy to my life.

This realization has been a crucial step in my journey towards self-acceptance and healing. It has allowed me to acknowledge my past mistakes and strive to be a better person, learning from my experiences and understanding the power of self-love and compassion.

So based on what I learned, here are seven steps to embrace vulnerability for personal growth and healing:

1. *Self-awareness:* Take time for introspection and self-reflection to understand the coping mechanisms and emotional walls built during childhood. Recognize how past experiences may be influencing current behavior and attitudes.

2. *Seek support:* Reach out to trusted friends, family members, or professional counselors to share your feelings and experiences. Talking about your pain can help alleviate the burden and foster emotional connection.

3. *Practice self-compassion:* Be gentle and forgiving with yourself. Acknowledge that it's okay to have flaws and vulnerabilities. Treat yourself with the same kindness and understanding you would offer to a loved one.

4. *Embrace vulnerability:* Allow yourself to be open and vulnerable with others, expressing your true emotions and needs. Vulnerability can lead to deeper connections and foster authentic relationships.

5. *Challenge negative self-talk:* Identify and challenge the negative thoughts and beliefs that perpetuate feelings of inadequacy and self-hate. Replace them with positive affirmations and empowering self-talk.

6. *Take responsibility:* Acknowledge your role in shaping your life and take responsibility for your actions. Avoid blaming others or external circumstances for your current situation.

7. *Seek professional help if needed:* If you find it challenging to navigate your emotions or past trauma, consider seeking the support of a therapist or counselor who can guide you through the healing process.

By following these steps, individuals can gradually transform their perspective and embrace vulnerability as a source of strength and growth. Through self-awareness, support, and self-compassion, one can break free from the confines of the warrior persona and begin a journey towards embracing authenticity and finding brilliance within. In tune with 'stop-living-in-fear' I am stepping out and devoting my life to service people – to see their fears and feed their light. Let them see the light that is in them. We are not bound by other people's opinions and our past experiences. Now don't get me wrong, God has been good to me and that is what clicked to me. If God is on my side when I am on autopilot mode, what could my life look like if I also took the yoke aka the steering wheel of the plane and was flying the plane. There is no limit.

I have found my purpose in helping people uncover their brilliance and embrace vulnerability. In this moment of triumph, I have realized that my true success lies not in titles or achievements, but in the profound impact I have on the lives of others.

And so, the warrior within has been repurposed, accompanied by a brilliant soul who shines with authenticity, compassion, and resilience. As I continue to evolve and share my light with the world, I know that my journey has only just begun—a journey of love, growth, and the ever-expanding embrace of vulnerability. I will embrace the process, stay curious and be open to the lessons that life has to offer.

About Stacey

Stacey Pitcher, a native of the beautiful island of Bermuda, has always been driven by a deep desire to make a positive impact on people's lives. After completing her bachelor's degree in Finance at the University of Western Ontario and earning an MBA from Keller Graduate School of Management – DeVry University, she went on to become a Certified Public Accountant (CPA). Her career in the accounting field began with Audit at PricewaterhouseCoopers, where she honed her skills and gained valuable experience.

Throughout her career, Stacey's passion for helping others never wavered. For two years, she served as the Treasurer at the Women's Resource Centre, dedicating her time to support and empower women in her community. Although she achieved success in the accounting industry, Stacey felt a deep yearning to follow her true passion—to help people thrive and embrace their unique brilliance.

Driven by this calling, Stacey founded 'Flawed Brilliance Coaching, Mentoring, and Consulting.' This transformative business is built on the belief that everyone possesses inherent imperfections and unique brilliance that can be harnessed to achieve personal and professional growth. Through a holistic approach, Flawed Brilliance empowers clients to overcome challenges, unlock their true potential, and embrace their authentic selves.

As a coaching and mentoring consultant, Stacey tailors her services to meet the specific needs of each individual or organization. Whether it's one-on-one coaching, group mentoring, or consulting sessions, her focus is on providing comprehensive support and guidance.

Stacey's journey has been one of continuous learning and growth. From her early days in Audit at PricewaterhouseCoopers to becoming a Senior Accountant at Enstar Group Limited and later an Assistant Director at the Bermuda Monetary Authority, she gained valuable insights and experience in the financial sector. Additionally, she served as a Finance Consultant at Arch Reinsurance, demonstrating her versatility and adaptability in various roles.

Despite her successful career in accounting, Stacey always knew that her true calling was to help others embrace their flaws and discover their brilliance. With Flawed Brilliance, she found a way to merge her expertise in finance with her passion for personal growth and empowerment.

Beyond her professional achievements, Stacey remains deeply committed to giving back to her community. Her work at the Women's Resource Centre reflects her dedication to supporting and uplifting others, especially women facing challenges in their lives.

Stacey Pitcher's story is a testament to the power of following one's passion and creating a business that aligns with one's purpose. As she continues to empower individuals and organizations through Flawed Brilliance, Stacey's impact on the lives of others grows stronger. Through her coaching, mentoring, and consulting services, she is helping others find their light within, embracing their flaws, and unleashing their true brilliance to create a brighter future.

In addition to her remarkable journey in the world of finance and personal growth, Stacey Pitcher's life is beautifully complemented by her adorable four-legged companion, Kaili – her charming Morkie (a delightful Maltese-Yorkshire Terrier mix) who holds a special place in Stacey's heart.

Learn more at:

- www.flawedbrilliance.org

CHAPTER 14

FUEL FOR THE SOUL: KINDLING THE PASSION TO SERVE

BY MICHAEL MIKLAUS

To revisit a place or a feeling you must first have already been there. Most people, when asked to define success, usually default to storybook examples of monetary excess or fame. That is because most people have self-limiting beliefs within themselves. We all have a positive – 'I think I can' voice, and a negative – 'Who are you kidding, you are an imposter' voice. Often, we let the loud negative, self-limiting voice within become a bully over our lives. It becomes easier to cast excuses on the cloaks of others perceived successes. Then you can employ the self-defeating practices of comparison and envy, rather than take the opportunity for a little meditation and self-examination.

Money and fame, at the end of the day, are both illusory at best. True success in this life is better measured by what contributions you make to help improve the lives of others.

When I was twenty years old, I left UCLA after two short quarters and went to work for a Savings and Loan in the San Fernando Valley. These thrifts were also known as Savings Banks in other parts of the country. Some were federally-chartered mutual institutions, not unlike a credit union, owned by their savers. The primary purpose of Savings and Loan was to promote thrift and home ownership. An opportunity to help people save money and borrow to secure a home for their families felt good to me. At the time, I could not explain why, but it was important to me to learn how to help someone buy a home. There is a success principle here. To excel, your primary life endeavor needs to be in alignment with your values and your gifts. My gifts are an understanding of complex financial ideas and an ability to simplify them and communicate them in a manner that builds clarity for others.

We all come from diverse backgrounds, economic levels, and childhood experiences. For many, the circumstances you grew up in may still define your reality. You allowed it. The key is we all start from somewhere, however humble the conditions. Where we finish our life journey and how we get there is our choice. I made the choice to learn all I could about banking, marketing, and home lending. I took every class offered to me, bought and read books, and looked for mentors willing to answer my questions. I drove two nights a week to the American Savings and Loan Institute classes held on Spring Street in downtown Los Angeles from my apartment in Orange County. My goal at the time was simple enough. Prove to myself and my family that this college dropout could become successful in banking.

I will never forget taking my mom out to lunch for her birthday. I was twenty five and I had just accepted an offer to join San Diego Federal Savings and Loan as a regional branch manager in Sacramento, CA. During lunch I asked if she was proud of me. Her response? She hoped she could be someday. It would have stung less if she had reached across the table and slapped me. In time, I was able to reflect on this meeting as a gift. Never trust your value as a person to anyone else's judgement. Sometimes our relatives and closest friends can keep us mired in the quicksand of our shared circumstance. They, through transference, place their own seeds of negativity and doubt into your mind, or help you to water and grow the seeds of self-limitation already thriving within you. Simply put, do not ask for directions to a successful life from someone who has not been to the destination.

This feels to me like a wonderful time to discuss mindset. The best decision making comes from our mind being neutral and detached from the outcomes. Tremendously successful people have this mindset. Faith in God is an integral part of the foundation of a healthy mindset. We all want to belong, to be loved, and to be accepted. Family: Caring for and supporting others is also a value I believe is embedded in our very nature. Health: Without it, you have nothing.

A successful life journey requires a proper mindset. I am 100% responsible for my life. I am 100% responsible for my own growth as a human. I am 100% responsible for my future – this starts now. This then needs to be manifested in your daily practices. Start each day by expanding your mind. Read faithfully non-fiction books on any subject you desire to explore or learn about. Spend a few minutes on reflecting, meditation, or prayer. The focus is gratitude. Then get up and exercise. Exercise is a difference maker. You cannot feel worse from exercise. A good sweat is a byproduct of staying healthy. These practices help me start each day with a positive open mindset and a healthier outlook. You cannot begin your day with negativity and be open to growth.

At the end of the workday, I hold myself accountable. You can too. Ask, did you fully apply yourself today to important activities adding value to others? Was your effort today worthy of your best version of you? Now, do not stop here. You have a home life and personal relationships. The people you care about deserve the best version of you as well. Be present for the ones you love.

Do you know your gifts? Have you ever asked yourself what drives or motivates you? What would you do if you could, where to be paid was simply icing on the cake? René Rodriguez in his book, *Amplify your Influence,* explains that we each have a story in us that explains our why. Mine started at nine when my mom and dad got divorced. My mom, looking to validate herself by acceptance from others, bounced with us kids in tow, in and out of unhealthy relationships until she met my stepdad. He married my mom, provided a home for her, and showed grace to her, and at this point, to her five children. The youngest, my newest brother, was his only child. I was now the oldest of five.

The security of a home, and all it represented became a pillar in my values. I now know why promoting thrift and home ownership resonated with me. It has driven my desire to focus on how I can add value to the lives of others You too, have a life story or event that impacts, good or bad, who you are today.

I chased recognition and material success until I was almost forty. I became, in my thirties, Executive Vice President and Chief Operating Officer of a local thrift. We grew from nine offices and one hundred and fifty million dollars in assets, to thirty-five offices from

Sacramento to San Jose. We had eight hundred million in assets and a billion dollars in loans serviced for others. I took part in the first multi-thrift collateralized mortgage obligation. These are commonly called mortgage-backed bonds today. I was a regular guest on local radio and the TV news, as an expert to explain interest rate changes, and their impact on housing affordability. The less involved I was with helping clients, the more I felt like an empty suit. While I was prominent in the community, my personal relationships suffered. I was still there and doing things with and for my kids, but at times I wasn't present.

I left the bank and first consulted with other local banks and mortgage brokering. I sold commercial real estate. Then, because of a call from the Federal Home Loan Bank of San Francisco, I was hired to become the President of a small insolvent savings bank the FSLIC did not have sufficient funds to close.

I discovered I loved being back in the bank lobby talking to depositors and borrowers. When a client came in with a mortgage question, or desire to buy a home, I was able to help them, coach them and explain to them their loan choices. This self-discovery led me to decide to give up the security of a bank title for the joy of being a loan advisor. Loan officer positions became fewer and fewer during this period of bank failures and consolidations. Two new avenues for a home buyer emerged. The mortgage banker and the mortgage broker.

I attended a men's Christian Leadership conference in Oakland, CA. in 1996 called Promise Keepers. Being surrounded in the Oakland A's stadium by men showing vulnerability, admitting their failings as dad's and husbands, and praying together to do better was very affirming. I felt restored, blessed, and ready to serve others. On the way home, I decided to start my own mortgage company. The word that kept coming into my head and stirring my heart was the need to live with integrity in all matters professional and personal. The lesson was simple. If you are unfulfilled where you are, work to improve it, or leave and start over. It is never too late to begin anew.

When charting a course in a new direction, you must go all in. There cannot be a Plan B. A divided mind will not help you persevere or guide you to the correct choices once outside your comfort zone. By the following year, Integrity Mortgage was born. I soon realized people do not pay you for your wisdom or your knowledge. They first desire to be heard and then they willingly pay you for what you do for them. Home loan rates are remarkably similar no matter who is the provider. The task of a true mortgage broker is to be able to become the client's trusted mortgage advisor. Then your knowledge is worthy of a price.

I also found myself growing as a person again. My original ideas of success were fading out of my life like fools' gold lost in the twilight. I learned there is no real satisfaction in measuring dollar outcomes. A true form of accountability is to measure my daily actions and efforts by serving others. My freedom comes in the discipline. False accountability would say if our goal were to fund twenty million dollars and we only funded nineteen million dollars we failed. What if my goal, instead, is to help one hundred families achieve home ownership or more favorably restructuring their mortgage debt. Then, if we only helped ninety three families, we are still a success because of the service we provided to the families we advised. Clearly transactions bring in income. When we serve our clients well our income is assured.

More important, by treating the close of escrow as chapter one in our client relationship we become a true mortgage advisor by staying in their sphere of advisors. The law of attraction dictates how to become referable. Clients must respect, know and like you. First, you must show you know and like them, and desire to still add value to their lives. I do not want to be a typical mortgage loan officer that 'closes the deal' and is soon forgotten.

My passion is to make certain my clients understand the payment they can afford. This may not be their desired payment. I want to teach them the use of leverage to accumulate wealth through a home purchase. I pray we have properly advised them about reserves and how to stay financially secure when life deals them a setback. I want our clients to feel safe that they can ask every question. Only then, with their referrals and repeat business do we earn the privilege of being their trusted mortgage advisor.

Today, I am over seventy. I have been happily married now for almost twenty years to my wife Cynthia. She is my partner, friend, lover, sounding board and cheerleader. She is an amazing host to our friends, clients, and family. She is always a kind, patient ear to our eight kids and ten grandchildren. We find joy in cooking together, relaxing at home together, going on short trips and planning social gatherings in our home and backyard. She makes me a better version of myself. We are financially secure and practice the same money principles I try to share with others.

I love and value my realtor friends. I approach each new day with a passion to serve. When asked how to be a referral-based business, I explain the power of questions and listening actively to the answers. I have trained my team here at Integrity to coach other mortgage advisors and realtors desiring to serve to be problem solvers. Listen to the answers of clients for:

- Changes in their lives
- Points of pain or circumstances of pleasure
- Life changes
- Diplomas, diapers, divorce, relocation, a need to downsize. and more are only discovered by listening

We teach how to stay connected and be a part of their client's lives.

Then they can be of service when offering choices to solve for the changes that occur over time in everyone's lives. This is my vision of a life successfully lived: *Service beyond self with a growth mindset.*

To learn to grow you must be teachable. To find freedom, a true form of success, you must have daily disciplines. True success is found in the joy of the daily activities in front of you. True success is to be with others who mirror your values and are willing to hold you accountable for your best version of yourself.

I feel joy in my plans and my daily actions. I am grateful for today. I am no longer attached to outcomes. I understand success requires occasionally failing. These are moments to be viewed as lessons for growth.

I am a knowledgeable mortgage advisor. My company and my team share my values. We supply advice on what is for most people the largest debt of their lives. Together we have built Integrity Mortgage with a focus on teaching people the right things to look for and what questions to ask.

I still see that displaced nine-year-old in my past. He is now safe and secure, grateful, and approaches each day with a mindset of abundance. He finds joy in hearing the stories of clients, helping others and lives a life rich in love. He has a sense of purpose. He would enjoy the opportunity to hear your story.

About Mike

Recognized as the National Association of Mortgage Brokers Mortgage Broker of the Year in 2022 and 2023. Mike Miklaus provides professional mortgage services and advice to homebuyers and property owners throughout the State of California. Mike's storied background and vast lending experience places him among the top mortgage brokers licensed in California. He has helped thousands of borrowers since starting Integrity Mortgage in 1996. His advice and counsel are sought after by realtors, other lenders, and clients alike.

Acknowledged by his peers as a leader in the mortgage industry, Mike has received many awards and recognitions. He was awarded Best of the Best and a top 1% in the industry by UWM, the largest lender in the country. He has completed certification through the Mortgage Mastermind Elite Coaching Program. He has also been a participant in the High Trust Sales Academy. He has been named a recipient of the Five Star Award in *Sacramento Magazine* on three occasions for his high client ratings and the lending experience provided to clients by his team at Integrity Mortgage.

As the President and Broker for Integrity mortgage, Mike still actively consults with clients. Using highly-valued tools and analytics, Mike and his team provide advice, not just price, to help borrowers make sound financial choices for their families. He partners with successful realtors to get loans approved quickly and escrows closed in a timely manner. Once the client takes possession, his team continues to add value and information so that borrowers can successfully manage their debts and enjoy the wealth obtained through homeownership.

Mike is an often-requested media expert on mortgage interest rates and housing trends in his immediate market in Northern California. He has appeared on local NBC, CBS, ABC and Fox affiliate stations as well as numerous interviews for local news and real estate show radio broadcasts. He has published articles about Real Estate and Lending in *Comstock Magazine* and *Executive Place Magazine*. He is a sought-after speaker by realtor groups, title companies, and service clubs.

When Mike is not assisting homeowners or referral partners, Mike can sometimes be found on a baseball diamond umpiring a community college or high school baseball game. This unique vocation began when Mike started umpiring youth baseball over thirty years ago. He is an avid swimmer; loves to snow ski and he enjoys taking walks with his wife Cynthia.

Mike and Cynthia enjoy short trips, day hikes, wine tasting, touring botanical gardens and hosting gatherings in their home. They love investing time with their children and grandchildren.

Highly approachable, you can contact Mike at:

- https://linktr.ee/mmiklaus

CHAPTER 15

THE ART OF OVERCOMING ADVERSITY

BY DR. PRITESH LOHAR

Success is walking from failure to failure with no loss of enthusiasm.
~ Winston Churchill

I remember that early spring day vividly, with me starting off in a great mood to finish off the week, but by the end of the day, calamity had struck. Much akin to a person who leaves his house for work and never comes back, because he has had a fatal accident. The only difference was that I was dead in all ways, except physically. That night and many more subsequent nights, all I wanted to do was shrink away and hide from the world, including myself.

Many of you reading this may have gone through such a harrowing, fearful and disastrous experience yourself. Nothing made sense, and yet in some strange sort of way, it finally made sense. My 'successful' life was only leading me on a path towards disaster. Despite achieving it all, I was living a spiritually dead life. While I understood that there was a purpose behind all this and a Divine plan, I was way too scared of walking down this new path, and extremely anxious about my future. In hindsight, I am extremely grateful to God/Source/Universe for redirecting my future from my selfish gains, towards having me discover my true passion and purpose. I came here to this world to create my own experience. While the pain was unbearable at times, affecting my health adversely, it led me to coin a quote (loharlogic. com) – *Pain is inevitable...Suffering is a choice.*

While I was unsure what would be my fate next, I began to 'stumble' upon various masterclasses, webinars, courses towards self-discovery for improvement. These were all synchronicities, guiding me to my highest self, but only given to me by Source, when I got myself ready to receive these divine gifts and blessings. By the end, the trial by fire was over (because storms always end), I was a Certified Life Coach and a 6-Phase Meditation Trainer.

It took me several months of deep inner work and soul work to realize that I was finally free of everything that was holding me back. I want to highlight here how I came back successfully from a seemingly hopeless situation. My goal is to introduce and share the actions that I took to unshackle my bonds, and I sincerely hope these secrets can lead you to true success and happiness, despite your past failures, mistakes and rejections.

1) <u>Awareness and Acceptance</u> – This is where the healing and growth first started and pushed the other steps into action. I knew I had a problem, but when nothing negative happened, I found myself ignoring my habits, and living like I didn't have a problem. At the nadir of the downward spiral, I finally realized that I had a real problem, which I had been neglecting and minimizing all my life. Through the shame and guilt, I accepted that I had to change myself. Its almost like a light switch turning on in my inner darkness. I knew I could not make any changes until I accepted and felt inside me that I was not doing what my soul really wanted. Acceptance begins when you can look back and be ok with the fact that things happened as they did, that the pain is still there and probably be always there in some way, but that there are new things to capture my energy and attention, and that is okay, too.

2) <u>Empathy, Compassion and Self-Love</u> – These three are all interconnected, and in this troubling time, I had to read and learn how to go about it. It was vital for me to build a strong relationship with myself first, in order to foster personal growth and fulfilment. Despite my situation and my role in it, I began to treat myself with kindness and respect, and prioritizing my personal well-being. The goal was to cultivate inner strength and a healthier sense of self-worth. Self-care was paramount. The beauty was that I started to develop empathy and compassion towards people I lived or

interacted with. Relationships became healthier. I realized that the entire episode causing disappointment was a major turning point in my life, not a roadblock. Like Rumi said – *"I would like my life to be a statement of love and compassion....and where it isn't, that's where my work lies."*

3) <u>Gratitude and Forgiveness</u> – This can be the hard part if you think you have been in control of everything and everyone in your life. For me, I had expressed my gratitude in words before, but by daily journaling of gratitude towards small and big things, I felt like I was opening to the Universe to receive more blessings. It was difficult to stay resentful while being grateful. Forgiveness was the hardest part for me. As I learned the power of self-forgiveness and forgiving others for real or perceived hurts, I felt it easier to let go of my past. Living in the present became easier, and while there was always a concern about my future, it no longer had any power over me. I remember the words of C.S. Lewis – *"If God forgives us, then we must forgive ourselves, otherwise it's like setting up ourselves as a higher tribunal than Him."*

4) <u>Prayers, Faith and Spirituality</u> – I already was receiving signs that God was planning to provide for me during the struggles. People around me were exhorting me for prayers, I had a Psalm written on a stone for my birthday, and people around me were already talking to me about Jesus. In all honesty, I thought I was a prayerful person, but it was more mechanical, rather than a desire or habit. I had to ask people "How do you Pray?" and I never believe I prayed for other people before this. Once I started praying to God in my own imperfect way, I felt a strange peace among the fear, panic and anxiety. I started praying for others and asking God to remove blockages and obstacles from my path. The scientific truth is this – praying to God changes your brain chemistry. As Marshall Segal says – *"When God makes and carries out His plans for us, He plans for us to pray. The absolute sovereignty of God over every detail of our lives, is the hope and foundation for our praying."*

5) <u>Energy and Vibrations</u> – Everything in the Universe is interconnected and composed of energy. Vibrational frequencies are influenced by thoughts, emotions, intentions, and the surrounding environment. Vibrations typically involve the transfer of energy. I understood,

157

that before my difficult situation, my lower vibrations were co-existing with a negative energy transfer. It used to drain my energy interacting with people due to my thoughts and emotions. In the words of Abraham Hicks: *If there is something that you desire, and it is not coming to you, it means you are not a vibrational match to your own desire.* I learnt to use positive energy transfer, vibrating from a higher frequency. This led to a sense of harmony, spiritual growth and more fulfilment. Its important to stay grounded, protect your energy and vibrate higher.

6) <u>Connecting to Your Higher Self</u> – I started the process of deepening my connection with the wisest and most authentic aspect of my being. In short, apart from introspection, reflection, mindfulness and presence, I began to cultivate the art of listening to my inner voice. I started to pay more attention to the subtle thoughts, feelings and intuitive nudges within me. I began to trust my instincts and allowed my higher self in making choices aligned with my truest self. Connecting to my higher self also meant asking for help and protection, and guidance from angels, guides and masters. Connecting to your higher self is a deeply personal and spiritual journey. As Sanaya Roman says – *"The further away from your higher self you are, the harder things become, and the more intense and turbulent your emotions may be."*

7) <u>Mindset of Self-belief, Resilience and Perseverance</u> – My whole life had been relatively successful, despite having a negative mindset. I discovered the need to have a positive mindset, cultivating a constructive and optimistic outlook in life, even in the face of challenges. I began to develop this, along with a self-belief that I could achieve my goals, dreams and desires, through self-reflection, practice and surrounding myself with supportive and positive influences. This began to greatly influence my actions and outcomes in life. I have always been a resilient character and perseverance is my middle name. But this trial required me to raise my game. Both these qualities helped me overcome multiple challenges during this long trial and kept me driven and determined to keep going. I found out that the more I developed the muscle of these qualities, the more I was able to overcome even the toughest of circumstances. In the words of C.S. Lewis – *"Hardships often prepare ordinary people for an extraordinary destiny."*

8) <u>Letting go of Limiting Beliefs</u> – This is an empowering process that can positively transform your life. It began with me recognizing and acknowledging the beliefs that were holding me back. These were ingrained into me at a very early age, by family, friends and peers. The first step was reflecting on their origins and examining whether they were based on facts or simply perceptions. The next step was to consciously choose to challenge and replace these limiting beliefs with more empowering and supportive ones. Affirmations and seeking support from others were very helpful in this journey. This is a lifelong process, and change takes time and effort, but with persistence, it was possible to start to break free from these limiting beliefs and embrace a more expansive mindset.

9) <u>Intentional Living</u> – I don't know how many of us practice this, I certainly lived a scattered life with distractions and out of my alignment with my goals and values. Intentional living is about consciously and purposefully directing your actions, decisions and thoughts towards what truly matters to you. It involves being mindful of one's choices, values, and goals and aligning your daily life with them. To live intentionally, I started by clarifying my values and identifying what was most important for me. I set clear goals that reflected those values and began to create a roadmap to achieve them. I began to simplify my life by decluttering physical possessions, relationships and commitments that no longer served my purpose. I began to prioritize my time and energy on activities and relationships that brought me joy and growth. Remember that intentional living is an ongoing process. Every morning when you wake up, meditate on your conscious intentions for that day, and visualize every detail of how you want the day to unfold. Once you embrace the journey of intentional living, you will find yourself living a more meaningful and purposeful life.

10) <u>Calming Techniques</u> – Meditation, Deep Breathing and EFT – Stress, Panic and anxiety had been extreme for me during this trial. I used a combination of meditation, deep breathing and Emotional Freedom Techniques (EFT), as a comprehensive approach towards relaxation, stress reduction, and emotional well-being. EFT is a technique that combines acupressure and psychology to alleviate emotional distress by tapping on specific points of the body. Meditation helped me to enhance self-awareness, improve concentration, and promote

a sense of calm and inner peace. EFT helped me to release negative emotions, reduce anxiety, and address issues of trauma and phobias. Deep Breathing involves taking slow, deep breaths, focusing on the inhalation and exhalation, which helped me to calm the nervous system and promote a sense of relaxation. It's important to explore different approaches and find what works best for you in terms of stress management and emotional well-being.

11) Creative Visualization and Manifestation – These are practices commonly used to help individuals manifest their goals and desires. I always had good imagination, and creative visualization helped me to create a mental picture and scenario of what I wanted to achieve. By vividly visualizing my desired outcome, I engaged my mind and emotions, and helped align my thoughts and actions towards achieving a particular goal. Manifestation is the belief that I can attract and bring into reality, the things that I desire by focusing my thoughts, energy, and actions on them. That involved setting clear intentions, cultivating positive beliefs and taking inspired action to bring about the desired outcome. The goal is not to confuse the Universe about what you want. A word of caution – while creative visualization and manifestation are often used together, they are not magical solutions. You will require consistent effort, proactive behaviour and a positive mindset. It's also valuable to maintain realistic expectations while remaining open to possibilities and opportunities that may arise along your journey.

12) Abundance – refers to a state of having more than enough of something, whether its material wealth, opportunities, love or any other desired aspect of life. Who would not want that? The problem is there are people with abundance living with a mindset of lack, and then people like me, who realised abundance during perceived lack. I was really worried about my financial situation during this crisis, and yet my bank balance after one year was higher than when the crises started. And the surprising thing was that I was still able to afford whatever I needed (and sometimes whatever I desired). So, it is worth noting that abundance is a subjective concept, and it may mean different things to different individuals. It's important to define abundance in a way that resonates with you personally, and to approach it with a healthy and balanced mindset. Practices like gratitude, positive affirmations, visualization and conscious

intention setting can help cultivate a mindset of abundance. I am currently manifesting abundance, and I firmly believe I can have it all.

Success Re(defined): There is a saying that before something great happens to you, everything falls apart. I was never broken, it was my environment that was broken, and I reacted to that in the only way I knew how to survive. But underneath all that pain, I discovered how to thrive. By redefining success in a way that aligned with my values and priorities, I could create a more fulfilling and purpose-driven life that went beyond societal expectations. A successful life is more than a high-paying job, other external measure or admiration from peers. It takes account of your changed circumstances and liberates you from the need to achieve it all now. It allows you to set your own goals, find joy in the journey, and embrace a more holistic view of success that encompasses various aspects of well-being and personal satisfaction. Success in the face of adversity requires embracing failure as an opportunity for learning and growth and having the determination to keep moving forward despite setbacks or obstacles.

In the words of Winston Churchill again –

Success is not final; failure is not fatal;
it is the courage to continue that counts.

About Dr. Pritesh

Dr. PRITESH LOHAR, MD, FACP, is a Board-Certified Medical Oncologist and Haematologist. While successfully treating cancer patients for two decades, he finally found his true life purpose and passion. Being a Life Coach, changing limiting beliefs and uplevelling the mindset of his clients for personal and business growth and expansion is his mission.

While performing his clinical duties, he successfully became certified as a Life Coach and as a 6–Phase meditation Trainer by EVERCOACH and Mindvalley. Additionally, he is certified in Daniel Goleman's Foundational and Relational Skills of Emotional Intelligence. He is currently pursuing International Coaching Federation (ICF) credentialing and certification as a Professional Certified Coach (PCC). His areas of expertise and interest include Life Coaching, High Performance Coaching, Emotional and Spiritual Intelligence and Positive Psychology.

Dr. Lohar's goal is to impact as many lives (humans, animals and plants), positively as he can by imparting his coaching skills and life experience to others. His life experiences have taught him that 'Life is happening for me', and he believes imparting that experience and belief with as many individuals as possible, is beneficial to humanity. He is of the firm opinion that the best outcome for success comes in combining the scientific principles of the Universe along with spiritual teachings and experiences.

His approach to coaching is based on a foundation of empathy, active listening and non-judgment. He believes that everyone has unique talents waiting to be unleashed, and he is here to support and guide them in realizing their dreams and aspirations. Through personalized coaching sessions, he helps individuals cultivate self-confidence, enhance their communication skills, improve decision-making abilities, and create balance in various aspects of their lives. He focuses on areas such as self-awareness, goal setting, mindset shifts, and developing effective strategies to overcome obstacles.

He continues to practice Medical Oncology and provide his patients the compassionate care and healing that they need.

CHAPTER 16

DREAMS DRIVE SUCCESS ...NOT DOLLARS!
HOW ONE SMALL NICHE HEALTHCARE COMPANY SURVIVED 40 YEARS OF HEALTHCARE CHALLENGES

BY REGINE NEIDERS, PhD

Pain management programs – What are they?
Multidisciplinary and interdisciplinary pain management programs have been available to those with intractable pain since the 1960's. The first in the nation was at the University of Washington (circa 1960). There Dr. John J. Bonica (an orthopedist) established a program that considered the biopsychosocial aspects of chronic pain. He believed that a multidisciplinary approach in the course of 4 to 7 or more weeks, daily, would have the best possibility for success. The goal was the reduction of pain and a return to a more hopeful life. He included anesthesiology, psychology, physical therapy, and physiatry (physical medicine and rehabilitation).

Treatment was set up to meet the individual needs of each patient. Research protocols were initiated, and subsequently, with the help of Ronald Melzack, PhD and Patrick Wall, MD, the International Association for the Study of Pain (IASP) was established by 1973. The key objectives were and still are: "promoting research, education and clinical management of pain as well as fostering collaboration and networking among pain scientists and professionals across the world."

All entrepreneurs have a dream. In the early 1980's, four medical professionals (an orthopedist, physical therapist, psychologist and nurse case manager) found themselves treating the same chronic pain patients (injured workers) in each of their private practices. They were discussing the cases regularly and decided that a different approach was indicated. Each was aware of the work that was being done at the University of Washington. None of these professionals were financially dependent upon creating a new concept, so they could dream. They wanted to impact the trajectory for these chronic pain patients.

The plan was early intervention and multidisciplinary treatment (as early as possible after an injury). They were optimistic and excited and in 1984 founded **NW Spinal Rehabilitation**. They hired an office manager, a marketing professional, an exercise physiologist, a physical therapy assistant, a transcriptionist, a billing professional, a vocational counselor, a nurse/biofeedback therapist and a job developer.

How could they let the community know they were open for business and ready to intervene early in a patient's pain? The marketing professional developed brochures, pounded pavement and tried to convince physicians and vocational counselors to refer early. Ultimately, patients were referred steadily. However, rather than early intervention, they were often 5 – 10 years post injury, still lingering in the worker's compensation system. As the team developed the program it became clear that modeling it after the University of Washington's program was their best bet. They created an eight-week full-time program with functional/exercise components, health education classes, biofeedback and relaxation, psychological intervention, medication management, vocational counseling and job development.

While NW Spinal Rehabilitation was developing their program, many other competitors were looking at the same population. The first few years were a struggle but the group kept their dream, met with their staff weekly and chiseled together a tighter and tighter program. Although the dream was early intervention, the referrals for treatment that they received continued to be 5 – 10 years post injury in spite of educating the referral sources. How could they possibly help individuals with such chronic conditions? Was multidisciplinary enough? They decided to stay the course.

First Challenge: Their first challenge came in 1986 when it seemed they also needed business help. They hired a CEO who was from the vocational counseling community. With his guidance the dream became more focused. They changed their name to United Backcare, Inc , moved to Bellevue, Washington, and leased a 12,000 square foot building to specifications with an indoor pool. A robust pool program was added to the lineup of program options. The plan was to be the 'Cadillac' back care clinic in Washington State. They still focused on early intervention. They limited the population to the most frequent type of referral (chronic back pain). Then, the second major 'hiccup' occurred, the second challenge.

Second Challenge: Referrals even with marketing efforts began to drop to a point where expenses clearly exceeded income. How could they stay in business and treat patients?

By 1989, there were 46 programs in Washington State claiming to have some variation of a multidiscipline program for treating injured workers in chronic pain. Was it the level of competition that was impacting the business? They found out that another treatment program in the same city had opened with an almost identical name! Then followed conversations with that program, letters from attorneys and ultimately, they changed their name.

Third Challenge: However, the payer also added another challenge (the third challenge). Programs needed to decide whether they were going to be interdisciplinary like the University of Washington program. If yes, in order to receive payment they needed to be CARF-accredited (Commission on Accreditation of Rehabilitation Facilities-accredited), by the end of 1989. The good news was that United Backcare, Inc. already was following the University of Washington model. Now to learn what was involved in accreditation. Here again a lucky break occurred. A psychologist from the Midwest had just been hired and his boss from the hospital system there was willing to share their accreditation policies! Whew! The payer added one more hoop to jump through, negotiating contracts.

Over the next few years, the payer watched their monetary outflow to the 12 programs they had chosen. There were yearly maximums for how much they were willing to pay per program. If your business was flourishing and you billed more due to volume of patients than their maximum, they threatened to stop paying until the next year. The dream was teetering based upon economic concerns.

In 1990, referrals continued to diminish significantly, and the then CEO suggested that the four owners close down the program, as it was not viable and likely never would be.

Fourth Challenge: The original visionaries were in fact in debt. Their dream was crashing and they all agreed to the closure. Serendipitously, a small group consisting of the bookkeeper, the clinic administrator and her husband (a Boeing engineer) sat down and put together a proposal for keeping the program running. It included some layoffs, a plan for getting out of debt and a renewed commitment to building referral relationships and keeping the dream alive. Their proposal was presented to one of the founders who presented it to the remaining founders and they decided to give it another try.

The dream prevailed. The clinic administrator became the leader and a new era of tracking finances, paying back loans, keeping employees informed of the plans and the financials as well as always reviewing the dream, began. During this same time, the 12 accredited programs had quarterly meetings with the payer. The goal was to educate the payer about early intervention among other related topics. Many spirited exchanges occurred about the value of providing interdisciplinary treatment earlier, how to figure out outcomes and how to increase return to work as well as how to pay a fair amount for clinical services.

Fifth Challenge: Around 1994, the payer sent a letter to the 12 pain management programs stating that the programs had been interpreting their contracts incorrectly and each program owed up to $200,000 that would be taken off immediately while they treated patients. Once it was paid down they would receive reimbursement again. The pain programs hired an attorney who helped them negotiate with the payer. The result was that pain programs did not have to pay the money back (although all had already gone one or two month cycles with no reimbursement). Subsequently, two programs decided to close their doors, one in the north Puget Sound and one in south Puget Sound.

Sixth challenge: The Board and owners of United Backcare, Inc. looked at possible opportunities to provide their interdisciplinary services to more patients. They consulted with mentors and decided to open an evaluation-only clinic in Everett (north Puget Sound). This clinic evaluated patients and those that were appropriate for treatment were treated in Bellevue (a community 30 to 45 minutes from Everett at that time). After about 1 ½ years, referral sources began to complain that patients were not being treated in their community. The team decided to open a full clinic in Everett. Meanwhile the opportunity for a third clinic south of Bellevue became available, and a full clinic was opened in Puyallup (south Puget Sound).

Seventh challenge: In the year 1999, we had three clinics that were holding their own, we had a good reputation, we were staying true to our mission and vision, and we believed we could also help patients in Eastern Washington. The group's dreaming continued. We called up a few of our physician contacts in Wenatchee and discovered that the local hospital was looking into establishing a multidisciplinary pain management program. We secured an opportunity to present to the decision makers and ultimately they gave us their blessing to proceed. In 2000, we opened an interdisciplinary pain clinic in Wenatchee Washington. All looked rosy, however, we found there was a different culture in Eastern Washington that we had not considered before going there. Referral sources wanted to know that we had hired local staff, that ideally we were local and most importantly, that we understood the local economy. It was not as good east of the mountains as it was west of the mountains. Furthermore, the referral sources felt, if we were unsuccessful helping patients return to work and/or improving their pain, the same referral sources would be negatively impacted when seeing the patient's families at church, in the store, etc. They wanted outcome guarantees which we could not supply.

Eighth Challenge: During that time the payer was also making huge changes. They created a preferred provider system for physicians who wanted to be reimbursed by the payer. There were a handful of physicians who prescribed large amounts of opiates to their patients and also referred to pain management programs. Seven of these were no longer able to provide services to the payer's patients, therefore referrals from these providers dried up. At the end of four years we were not able to sustain the program due to staffing, referrals and finances. We closed our doors. A sad time for the dream in Eastern Washington. During the next decade we operated three locations. The dream was reviewed yearly and we agreed again and again that we wanted to provide earlier intervention in an interdisciplinary environment. However, new challenges lay ahead.

Ninth challenge: We still had a location in the middle of the Puget Sound. It was the location that had been built to specifications and created the name and vision United Backcare. Could we increase our reach if we changed our name and opened up to injuries other than back injuries? We decided with the encouragement of our Marketing Director to change our name to United Backcare, Inc. dba Pacific Rehabilitation Centers. Changing the perception of our referral sources was not an easy task. Economic patterns were changing around our Bellevue location. Bellevue was becoming an upscale city and injured workers could no longer afford to live there, even if they had been injured there. Traffic patterns began to change, also. More people moved into Bellevue for work with Nintendo, Google, Microsoft, Amazon, etc. Traffic became very heavy and commutes that had once taken half an hour to 45 min, were now an hour or more each way. Patients were unwilling to drive to Bellevue and as referrals dwindled we sadly shut our Bellevue doors in 2017. Could this dream survive?

Tenth challenge: The pandemic of 2020. What? …Another challenge? Close your clinics, keep your staff on payroll, and do what? Well… six of us got together and we developed the first completely virtual interdisciplinary CARF accredited pain management program in the nation! It only took us six weeks. We purchased equipment, we set up protocols for providing equipment to patients who did not have equipment, met with clinicians (on zoom) to alter and modify services, and using Zoom Medical, we restarted treatment. CARF accepted it and to this day we are able to offer this option to patients who live too far away to leave their farms or families for onsite treatment. Today treatment is four weeks full time (6 hours per day and 24 hours of follow-up) based upon the payers guidelines. We believe our optimism, creativity and willingness to forge ahead has kept us going, where others have closed. We still believe that, eventually, early intervention via interdisciplinary treatment will be accepted as part of treatment for pain.

CURRENT ENVIRONMENT

The current environment for multidisciplinary pain treatment varies from State to State. Over time, many programs in Washington State as well as others adopted the Commission on the Accreditation of Rehabilitation Facilities (CARF) guidelines for Interdisciplinary pain rehabilitation (IPR) treatment programs. Some states required CARF accreditation for payment of services. In the 1980's and 1990's there were over 300 accredited programs across the nation. With time and the change in medical interventions (e.g. interventionalists), pain programs began to lose their favor with insurance programs who wanted cheaper, less intensive approaches.

Today, (2023) there are 65 CARF-accredited interdisciplinary pain management programs left across the nation. Although the concept of multidisciplinary approaches to pain is still the standard based on the contribution of evidence-based practice, in reality, multidiscipline programs vary widely, some may see a patient individually and consult. Finding a comprehensive program with multiple disciplines is far more difficult. So how has Pacific Rehabilitation Centers (a private for-profit organization with a big dream) managed to maintain their multidiscipline services? Or have they?

First and foremost, caring, compassion and flexibility are our company's core values. Over the course of 39 years, we have been very fortunate to hire and attract professionals who have gone into the health care field because they want to make a difference. Those who then came to work for our company developed the belief that it is important to make a difference over the long haul (a lifetime) for chronic pain patients. They believe in our mission: To inspire and elevate through comprehensive treatment – one patient at a time. They all have agreed to the dream that early intervention is the goal and today our referrals are 1 – 1.5 years post injury as opposed to the 5 – 10 years at the inception of the company. We appreciate working together for the same outcomes and we like what we produce with our patients (life, work and wellness).

We are about making a substantive difference in a few people for a lifetime. In the course of 39 years we have treated over 10,000 people. Each was given the opportunity to fashion their future with our help! We have an incredibly loyal staff, some who have stayed with the company as long as 30 or more years. The bridge between the old and the new is alive and well. We look forward to another 40 years of challenges and eventually even 'earlier intervention for pain.'

About Regine

As a CEO of a small health care company for 33 years, Regine Neiders has worked with her company and staff to pivot and survive the healthcare changes in Washington State's Worker's Compensation system during that time.

Regine is a life-long learner who began her career path as a counselor for chronically mentally ill individuals. She worked in several mental health agencies, including a half-way house where individuals transitioned back to society. She realized that at the line level she was not able to effect change for the mentally ill population. Her next step was securing an MSW at the University of Washington in Seattle. She has always been interested in how organizations and systems change, and while there, specialized in Community Organizational Services. She also spent one year participating in a program called 'The Management Laboratory' where real life organizational/operational situations were brought to the group for discussion, planning, consultation and execution. She considers this one of her most impactful career experiences. She subsequently spent five years working in health care and decided that she needed to learn more in order to be a change agent.

Regine's next challenge was to complete her PhD in Social Welfare while beginning her career in chronic pain treatment. She strived toward leadership and wrote her dissertation thesis on returning injured workers in the Worker's Compensation system to work. She has been active in the Washington State Pain Interest Consortium where she is currently the Vice President. She was active in, and later the president of, the Industrial Rehabilitation Association of Washington for over ten years – until the organization merged with IARP (Industrial Association of Rehabilitation Professionals). Her goals have revolved around impacting payers for better evidence-based treatments for injured workers.

Regine has been invited to join, and has joined, several CEO groups where she has participated with other CEO's in making their organizations better functioning – based upon collective shared wisdom.

Regine has one stepson and three granddaughters all of whom she adores. She and her husband have a hobby farm where they grow vegetables, fruit and an assortment of flowers. They have been supporters of animal rescue organizations like the ASCPA during their entire 50-year marriage and have rescued five dogs to date.

Regine's next goal is to write about organizations like hers and provide thoughtful ideas for survival, growth and change.

Learn more about chronic pain at:

- www.pacificrehabilitation.com

CHAPTER 17

EMPOWER YOURSELF: RISING ABOVE LIFE'S CIRCUMSTANCES

BY DR. MARIA RODRIGUEZ

I didn't live with either of my parents. When they divorced, my dad sent us to the Dominican Republic. According to the story fueled by my dad, my mom didn't want me, preferred another man, and wanted us all dead. I always grew up with the idea that I had to fend for myself, to provide for myself. It was a very helpless, hopeless time. It took years to recover from the emotional damage my childhood did, and it came in a series of realizations that culminated in my starting the Care Counseling Center.

The truth is that life is a series of unpredictable twists and turns, and sometimes we find ourselves facing challenging circumstances that test our strength and resilience, no matter who we are. This is the basic foundation I start with when meeting any client, no matter who they are or how old they are.

However, no matter what life throws at us, we possess the power to overcome any adversity and create a life filled with happiness and fulfillment. By empowering ourselves, we can rise above the most demanding challenges, transform setbacks into opportunities, and emerge stronger.

Embrace Self-Awareness

The first step to empowerment is cultivating self-awareness. Reflect on your strengths, weaknesses, values, and beliefs. Understand your emotions and thought patterns. By clarifying who you are, you can make conscious choices and align your actions with your authentic self.

Shift Your Mindset

Your mindset plays a crucial role in your ability to overcome obstacles. Embrace a positive and growth-oriented mindset. Believe that you have the power to navigate through any situation. Reframe challenges as opportunities for growth and learning. Embrace a 'can-do' attitude and replace self-doubt with self-belief. Remember, your thoughts shape your reality.

Cultivate Resilience

Resilience is the key to bouncing back from adversity. Develop resilience by viewing setbacks as temporary and solvable problems. Build your inner strength by focusing on your ability to adapt and persevere. Seek support from loved ones and cultivate coping mechanisms such as mindfulness, gratitude, and self-care. Remember, resilience is not about avoiding difficulties but navigating them with grace and strength.

Set Goals and Act

Empowerment comes from setting goals and taking action toward them. Identify what you want to achieve and break it down into smaller, achievable steps. Set specific, measurable, attainable, relevant, and time-bound SMART goals. Create a plan and take consistent action towards your goals. Each small step forward will fuel your confidence and propel you closer to success.

Embrace Self-Compassion

In the face of challenging circumstances, it's essential to practice self-compassion. Treat yourself with kindness and understanding. Accept that setbacks and failures are a natural part of life's journey. Be gentle with yourself and practice self-care. Remember, you are deserving of love and forgiveness, both from others and yourself.

Seek Support and Build a Network

We are not meant to face life's challenges alone. Seek support from trusted friends, family, or mentors. Surround yourself with a positive and uplifting network that believes in your abilities. Engage in meaningful conversations and share your experiences. Collaboration and support will provide strength and encouragement on your journey to empowerment. Learn and Grow.

Empowerment is an ongoing process of learning and growth. Embrace a mindset of continuous improvement. Seek knowledge, explore new ideas, and challenge yourself to step outside your comfort zone. Read books, attend workshops, take courses, and learn from others' experiences. Each new lesson learned will expand your horizons and enhance your ability to overcome life's challenges.

Celebrate Your Victories

As you navigate through challenging circumstances and empower yourself, celebrate your victories. Recognize and acknowledge your progress, no matter how small. Celebrating milestones boosts your confidence and motivates you to keep moving forward.

Remember that true empowerment comes from within, no matter your life circumstances. By embracing self-awareness, shifting your mindset, cultivating resilience, setting goals, practicing self-compassion, seeking support, learning and growing, and celebrating your victories, you have the power to overcome any challenge that comes your way.

EMPOWERMENT IS THE STORY OF PERSISTENCE

Persistence is an important quality that can make a significant difference in achieving success and fulfillment in life. The unwavering commitment and determination to pursue goals and overcome obstacles, even in adversity. Persistence enables you to navigate through these obstacles with resilience and determination. It allows you to view setbacks as temporary roadblocks rather than permanent barriers, empowering you to find alternative solutions and keep moving forward.

Achieving Goals

Many worthwhile goals require time, effort, and perseverance. Persistence is crucial, whether building a career, starting a business, or pursuing personal growth. It helps you stay focused and committed to your objectives, even when progress seems slow, or obstacles appear insurmountable. With persistence, you increase your chances of achieving your goals and turning dreams into reality.

Building Resilience

Persistence and resilience go hand in hand. When you encounter setbacks or face failure, persistence keeps you going. It helps you bounce back, learn from your experiences, and try again. Each time you persevere through challenges, you develop resilience, strengthening your ability to handle future adversities with greater confidence and grace.

Learning and Growth

Persistence is a catalyst for continuous learning and growth. It pushes you beyond your comfort zone, encouraging you to explore new possibilities and acquire new skills. By persistently pursuing knowledge and seeking personal development, you expand your horizons, improve your abilities, and increase your chances of success in various aspects of life.

Cultivating Discipline and Determination

Persistence requires discipline and determination. It instills a strong work ethic and a commitment to follow through on your intentions. By practicing persistence, you develop consistency, perseverance, and self-control, essential traits for achieving long-term success.

Inspiring Others

When other people witness your persistent efforts and determination, you become a source of inspiration and motivation. Your example demonstrates that challenges can be overcome with dedication and perseverance. By inspiring those around you, you create a ripple effect of positivity, encouraging others to pursue their dreams and overcome their obstacles.

Fulfillment and Satisfaction

A unique sense of fulfillment and satisfaction comes from persistently working towards your goals. Knowing that you have given your best effort and remained steadfast in the face of difficulties brings a deep sense of accomplishment. The journey becomes rewarding and meaningful even if the outcome isn't exactly as planned.

Is it worth comparing ourselves to others? Not at all. We should never compare ourselves to others, no matter who they are. We all have our unique circumstances.

Comparing ourselves to others is a common human tendency driven by social influences and the desire for validation. However, constant comparison can harm our well-being and hinder personal growth. Those comparisons are like climbing an endless ladder – by the time you reach the top rung, more will be added, and the climb will continue when self-belief works us gradually to the top like an elevator.

SETBACKS — THEY CAN AND WILL HAPPEN

Dealing with setbacks requires a compassionate and forgiving approach toward ourselves. To navigate setbacks and forgive ourselves, we can acknowledge our emotions, embrace self-compassion, reframe our perspective, learn from experience, and focus on personal growth.

By practicing self-forgiveness, we release guilt, cultivate resilience, and open ourselves up to new opportunities for progress and success. Remember, setbacks are an inherent part of life, and through forgiveness, we can embrace them as valuable lessons on our journey.

Life's journey is the adjustment of realizing that nobody's path is linear; that happiness is a winding path of the good and the bad. We're supposed to experience sadness, too – because that can fuel growth and, more importantly, appreciate the truly happy moments in life.

Take Time for Yourself

Take 30 minutes…every day. Think about what's making you sad, what's making you angry, and what's making you happy, the trifecta of emotions.

Focus your energy on finding solutions for the problems affecting your life and how to amplify what's bringing in joy. It may not be an easy realization to make, as I've seen in my practice; some of us are so used to living unhappily that we no longer know how to be happy – because we know happiness, at some point, will end. The open secret is, though, the time and energy spent to understand growth will be worth it.

After 30 minutes, it's time to continue with the day, no more time to dwell on what's lurking in the shadows of your mind.

THE POWER OF SMALL STEPS: BUILDING TOWARDS BIG GOALS

When faced with a daunting challenge or a long-term goal, it's easy to feel overwhelmed and uncertain about where to begin – I see it in my practice every day. However, by embracing the concept of setting small goals that build towards a larger objective, you unlock a powerful approach to problem-solving and personal growth. Breaking down a big goal into smaller, manageable steps makes it more attainable, fuels motivation, builds momentum, and instills a sense of achievement.

Let's explore why picking small goals to build towards one significant goal is the best way to approach any problem.

Overcoming Overwhelm

Large goals can seem intimidating and overwhelming, causing us to feel paralyzed or discouraged before we begin. However, we shift our focus to manageable tasks by breaking them down into smaller goals. Each small step becomes less daunting, allowing us to move forward with confidence and clarity.

Building Motivation and Momentum

Small goals serve as building blocks for motivation and momentum. We experience a sense of accomplishment and fulfillment when we achieve these smaller milestones. Each success fuels our motivation and propels us forward, creating positive momentum that keeps us engaged and excited about the journey toward the larger goal.

Fostering Consistency and Discipline

Consistency and discipline are essential ingredients for success. By setting small goals, we establish a framework for regular progress. Consistently working towards these smaller targets builds discipline and reinforces positive habits. It helps us stay focused, committed, and accountable to ourselves, increasing the likelihood of achieving the ultimate goal.

Celebrating Achievements

Celebrating achievements, no matter how small, is crucial for maintaining motivation and boosting self-confidence. We can acknowledge our progress and celebrate our efforts with each small goal accomplished. These celebrations create positive reinforcement and reinforce the belief that we can achieve the larger goal.

Flexibility and Adaptability

Life is unpredictable, and circumstances may change along the way. Setting small goals allows for greater flexibility and adaptability. We can reassess and adjust our approach, ensuring we stay aligned with our overarching objective. This adaptability enables us to respond to challenges, seize new opportunities, and find alternative pathways toward our desired outcomes.

Picking small goals to build towards a larger goal is a transformative approach to problem-solving and personal growth. By breaking down overwhelming tasks, we empower ourselves to tackle any challenge with confidence and resilience. Remember, the small steps pave the way for significant accomplishments and bring us closer to our most ambitious dreams.

EMBRACE YOUR INNER CEO: TAKE CHARGE OF YOUR LIFE'S SUCCESS

Life is a grand adventure, and you have the incredible opportunity to be the CEO of your journey.

Step 1: Define Your Vision

Every remarkable CEO starts with a clear vision for their organization.

Similarly, you need to define your vision. Take a moment to envision the life you desire—your dreams, aspirations, and core values. What do you want to achieve? How do you want to impact the world? When you have a well-defined vision, it becomes your compass, guiding your actions and decisions.

Step 2: Set Strategic Goals

A CEO sets strategic goals to steer their company's growth. Likewise, set meaningful and achievable goals to shape your personal growth and progress. Create goals that align with your vision and break them down into smaller, manageable steps. Embrace the SMART goal-setting approach—specific, measurable, attainable, relevant, and time-bound. These goals become the roadmap to your success.

Step 3: Take Ownership of Your Actions

A CEO takes full ownership of their actions and decisions. Similarly, accept responsibility for your life. Recognize that you have the power to make choices that shape your future. Embrace the idea that no matter the circumstances, you always have a say in how you respond. Take control of your thoughts, emotions, and actions. Transform setbacks into opportunities for growth and learning.

Step 4: Cultivate a Growth Mindset

A CEO understands that growth and adaptability are essential for success. Develop a growth mindset—believing your abilities can be cultivated and improved. Embrace challenges as opportunities for learning and personal development. Embrace failure as a steppingstone toward growth. Emphasize self-improvement, learning from others, and embracing new experiences. Your mindset will determine the height of your achievements.

Step 5: Nurture Self-Discipline

Effective CEOs possess the discipline to lead their companies toward success. Cultivate self-discipline in your life. Create daily habits and routines that support your goals and vision. Prioritize tasks that align with your purpose and eliminate distractions.

Step 6: Seek Knowledge and Wisdom

Successful CEOs are lifelong learners, continuously seeking knowledge and wisdom. Feed your mind with a thirst for knowledge. Read books, attend seminars, take courses, and seek mentors who inspire and challenge you. Embrace new perspectives and expand your horizons. The more you learn, the more empowered you become to navigate life's challenges.

Step 7: Build a Supportive Network

CEOs surround themselves with a reliable network of advisors and mentors. Similarly, surround yourself with a supportive network of individuals who believe in you and your dreams. Seek mentors who have achieved what you aspire to accomplish. Connect with like-minded individuals who share your values and goals. A strong network provides guidance, accountability, and inspiration.

Step 8: Embrace Resilience and Take Calculated Risks

CEOs understand that resilience and calculated risks are essential for growth. Embrace resilience as you face obstacles and setbacks. Learn from your failures and use them as steppingstones toward success. Take calculated risks that align with your vision and goals. Embrace the unknown and step outside your comfort zone. Remember, outstanding achievements often require taking bold leaps of faith.

Just like a Chief Executive Officer steers a company towards greatness, you possess the power to take charge of your life, make impactful decisions, and shape your destiny. By embracing your role as the CEO of your life, you can unlock your full potential and create a life filled with purpose, fulfillment, and success.

I'VE BEEN THERE TOO

Returning to my childhood, I knew I would have to take the steps to care for myself. No matter how hard I worked after growing up and leaving the Dominican Republic, I struggled with my self-confidence. It's about finding the space and knowledge to love yourself, for what is already in place and what you've got left to learn, no matter if you are a child or an adult.

About Dr. Maria

Dr. Maria Rodriguez is an accomplished mental health professional dedicated to a compassion-first approach to helping immigrant individuals, children, and families adapt and thrive in the United States. She is recognized as one of the Top 25 executives of New Jersey and a Global Outstanding Leader in Health Care.

Dr. Rodriguez has an extensive academic background which has been fortified with numerous accolades. With a master's degree in Clinical Psychology from William Paterson University and a Ph.D. in General Psychology from Capella University, she further solidified her expertise with 18 years of experience as an Adjunct Professor of Women's and Gender Studies and Psychology. Across her notable career, she has amassed over two decades of hands-on experience in mental health counseling, providing invaluable support to diverse populations.

As a first-generation American with Dominican parents, she has cultivated a deep understanding of the myriad of challenges immigrants face as they work toward realizing their ambitious goals in a new home. Her innate sense of hope for her community led her to establish the Care Counseling Center (awarded the Best of Somerville, New Jersey, in 2022 and 2023) – a safe space providing support for emotional trauma, legal complexities, and practical issues that immigrants may face in addition to helping families and individuals from various backgrounds.

Today you can reach Dr. Maria for in-person and virtual wellness services centered on resolving conflicts in self, business, and relationships via her websites:

- MariaRodriguez.org
- CareCounselingCenter.org

CHAPTER 18

PURPOSE DELAYED BUT NOT DENIED
A JOURNEY TO SELF-LIBERATION

BY ELIZABETH AGUILERA

If nothing changes, nothing changes. If you keep doing what you're doing, you're going to keep getting what you're getting.
You want change, make some.
~ Courtney C. Stevens

For three years in a row, I watched the 4th of July fireworks through the same window, in the same room of the same house, in the same pain, with the same tears silently streaming down my face. As I held my son tightly, I realized, in that profound moment, that I had to save myself. No one else could rescue me, but me. I knew I would release the hounds of hell when I asked for the divorce, but I was finally ready to fight for myself, for my son, and for the life of peace I longed for and knew was waiting for me on the other side of this suffering.

I know what it feels like to be trapped in a life you never wanted.

I endured 16 agonizing years in a toxic relationship with an overt narcissist, half of which were spent in a suffocating marriage, until the day I realized staying was killing my soul. The day I finally acknowledged that staying was snuffing out my life force, there was no turning back. I knew I had to get out. For years, fear paralyzed me, shame crippled me, and I was clueless about how I ended up there or how to escape. The fear was so overwhelming that I failed to see the open door to my freedom that had always been there.

Leaving a narcissist is far from easy; it felt like experiencing the ten plagues of Egypt simultaneously. However, leaving wasn't just a conscious decision to distance myself from the toxicity, it was an act of pure survival. The moment I put myself first and said, *"I choose me"*, a peace that surpasses all understanding washed over me.

Even though we divorced when my son was 6, the narcissist did everything in his power to make my life a living hell until my son turned 18, and I could legally sever all ties. At the time, I lacked the language to describe the torment I endured. The term 'narcissist' wasn't commonly used in the 1980s. All I knew was that he reveled in intentionally and relentlessly hurting me. Unaware that I was dealing with a narcissist, I fell for every trick in his manipulative playbook:

- He isolated me from friends and family, always demanding to be first.
- He thrived on instigating conflicts.
- He mentally and emotionally drained me to the point of exhaustion.
- He callously disregarded my obvious unhappiness.
- He exuded arrogance and condescension, believing he was better than everyone.
- He adamantly refused counseling.
- He attempted to gaslight me, making me question my sanity while insisting that I was the problem.
- He deliberately baited me and engaged in twisted games.
- He was an insatiable black hole; no matter how much energy, attention, or time I gave him, it was never enough.

The narcissist's ultimate goal was to make me surrender in every situation. Every time I went along to get along, I silenced my own voice and disappeared a little more until I became invisible. For those of us who have fallen into the narcissist's trap, it's essential to redefine relationship success and realize that healthy ones will foster your independence and encourage you to grow.

Reflecting on my journey, there are five pieces of advice I would share with my younger self to avoid the drama in my love life:

1. Never prioritize another person over yourself. As Socrates wisely stated, "To know thyself is the beginning of wisdom." Engage in inner work: self-exploration, self-reflection, personal growth, understand your limits, and stand firm when boundaries are challenged.

2. Retain your individuality and embrace what makes you uniquely you. Resist losing yourself in a relationship. Don't stop what you love to do! Healthy love allows you to flourish while maintaining your identity, never seeking to uproot you or change who you are.

3. Invest in yourself every day. Continuously expand your mind and feed your soul. Life is a constant journey of growth or decline; there is no in-between.

4. Always set new goals for yourself. Life is so much more exciting when you are working towards something! Whether big or small, setting goals makes life more fun, and it makes you more intriguing! You'll always have something to talk about, people will want to know what you're up to, and who knows whom you'll inspire just being authentically you?

5. Embrace opportunities that foster personal growth. Say 'yes' to new experiences, invitations, and opportunities that both excite and scare you. Real growth doesn't happen within your comfort zone.

Looking back on my journey, I am grateful for the lessons learned from that relationship. It taught me to advocate for myself, establish boundaries, and prioritize my well-being. I redirected the wasted energy on the narcissist's games—replaying his hurtful words and deeds, believing his lies, and falling into emotional traps—into rebuilding myself and creating a life filled with love and genuine connections. I shifted my focus towards what I wanted and repeatedly chose myself until his presence faded into insignificance.

The countdown to Jamaica had begun again! I couldn't wait to run away to my 'happy place' and remember how to smile, laugh, and have fun again. Visiting once a year was no longer enough to make me feel better! I had to literally leave the country to find peace, to disconnect from being available for work 24/7, and to center myself so that I could go back to the chaos my life had become. I did find peace and happiness while I was away! Why couldn't I hold onto them once I went back home?

Jon Kabat-Zinn's book title, *Wherever You Go, There You Are*, became my mantra. The countdown to my annual trips to Jamaica, my sanctuary for mental well-being, reminded me that I sought solace in a place while failing to carry it within myself. I yearned to escape the constant demands of work that consumed me. I longed to permanently hold onto the inner peace I found on vacations but eluded me in everyday life.

I was trapped in a joyless job and career that felt inherently wrong. Golden handcuffs kept me tied to a place where I didn't belong. At the same time, fear of the unknown and resistance to change blinded me to other possibilities. For 30 years, I toiled in corporate IT, with the last two decades consumed by misery. I devoted myself wholeheartedly to the company, sacrificing everything for a paycheck and benefits. Yet, no matter how much I gave, it was never enough. The company consistently outsourced IT positions, and the constant fear of losing my job drained me of happiness for 20 years. My physical and mental health took a heavy toll during this long period of waiting. I didn't recognize who was looking back at me in the mirror.

Instead of taking control and seeking alternatives, I doubled down to become worthy of a job I didn't like and became a victim of my circumstances rather than the heroine of my own story. Once again, I found myself trapped in a life I never wanted, needing to save my soul that was on life support.

This time, the Universe stepped in and liberated me from the insanity of my unsustainable life: I lost my job while was sitting on the beach in Jamaica. The irony of being severed from employment while in my 'happy place' did not escape me. It was a reminder that the peace I sought didn't reside *in* a place, I **was** the place.

In an instant, I lost my identity and financial stability. My entire career was erased, I was thrown in the garbage with yesterday's trash, and my 30 years of dedicated work were dismissed.

During my professional life, I consented to outdated corporate norms, even though I was suffering physically and mentally trying to live up to unrealistic expectations. I never questioned these norms, convinced that sacrifice was the price I had to pay for a salary and benefits. It's time for us to challenge these outdated, patriarchal corporate norms and start a movement rooted in wholeness and well-being, not on sacrifice and burnout. Let's redefine career success and show future generations that they need not lose themselves in service of career.

Reflecting on my journey, there are five pieces of advice I would offer my younger self to navigate the drama in my professional life:

1. Trust your instincts. If you feel out of place, *listen* to that inner voice. Do not suppress it. Embrace its message and find peace within it. Your intuition holds profound wisdom.

2. It's perfectly acceptable to stay where you are while simultaneously devising an exit strategy. Life isn't an either/or scenario; it's both/ and. You can acknowledge your current situation while actively working towards a brighter future.

3. Be clear about what you desire next and create a plan to pivot towards it. Yes, fear may accompany you on this journey, but forge ahead regardless. Embrace discomfort as an essential element of growth.

4. Understand that you won't always see the entire path laid out before you, and that's perfectly fine. Take the first step, and the subsequent steps will reveal themselves.

5. You did not sign up to endure workplace abuse or mistreatment. Set firm boundaries in your professional and personal life. This is an act of self-care and self-preservation.

Looking back on my journey, I'm deeply grateful to have learned that losing my job, career, and what I thought I wanted, was my liberation. I learned that once you do face your fear, it gets easier. You become stronger by standing in your power, seeing your options, and realizing you are the co-creator and author of your own life! I now approach life with an open mind, welcoming possibilities and embracing the unknown. I take action despite fear and uncertainty, understanding that everything I want awaits me beyond the confines of my comfort zone.

My journey towards redefining success began with the awareness that clinging to what I thought was security actually suffocated my existence. I decided to embark on unexpected and unfamiliar paths, granting myself permission to explore new territories. I extended grace and patience to myself, allowing time to unfold and reveal the direction I should take. I engaged wholeheartedly in inner work, healing old wounds, and forgiving past hurts. I learned to embrace humility, even when met with disapproval from those closest to me, standing firmly rooted in my faith and convictions. I willingly sacrificed everything necessary to progress towards my dreams.

I now undeniably embody success. The true gift lies not in external accomplishments but in my spiritual and personal growth. I measure success according to my degree of conscious awareness, my healing journey, and in my profound transformation. These intangible qualities have gifted me with peace and strength to fulfill my calling, regardless of fear or failure. I now live an authentic life on my terms, benefiting not only myself but also those around me. This synergy creates the ultimate win-win situation and defines my ultimate version of success.

As I transitioned from corporate life, I ventured into entrepreneurship and established my own business dedicated to helping seniors and overwhelmed Moms. After six years, I felt the familiar pull to 'more' within me. After months of feeling a pivot coming, I gave my two weeks notice and announced my departure to all my clients, leaving myself uncertain of what the future held. This decision sparked an accelerated journey of inner work, healing, awakening, training, education, and certification. It involved reconnecting with my faith, creating an entirely new life, and ultimately stepping into my purpose.

This pursuit of 'more' led me to become a certified Life Coach, an unexpected path that transformed my perception of myself and my capabilities. I discovered an entrepreneurial spirit I never knew existed within me – launching two businesses within six years. The person I once was now feels unrecognizable, and I am eternally grateful for that transformation.

I now realize that the most profound place I found myself trapped was within my own mind. My mindset was the primary source of my paralysis, preventing me from moving forward despite my desperate desire to do so. My limited thinking created a self-imposed cage that concealed potential opportunities from my sight. It was only through immense pain in my marriage and unexpected shifts in my professional life that I was forced to confront what my soul had been urging me to address all along. I learned that proactive decision-making and conscious creation of our desired lives yield far greater results. We always have a choice.

Reflecting on my journey, there are five pieces of advice I would offer my younger self to nurture her inner strength and prevent self-sabotage:

1. Self-love is the gateway to everything. Become your own best friend, treating yourself with care and compassion. Discover what brings joy to your heart, your passions, and what makes you smile. Engage in those activities regularly.

2. "Stand guard at the portal of your mind," Emerson eloquently said. Changing your thoughts is the catalyst for transforming your life. Watch your self-talk because you become what you think about.

3. Say 'yes' to what you truly desire. If you yearn for something, there must be a way to bring it to fruition. Ask yourself, "What step can I take to move me in the direction of my dreams?"

4. Cultivate a gratitude practice. Gratitude resonates with the frequency of abundance. It reminds you of the blessings already present in your life. Without appreciating what you have, how can the Universe trust you with more?

5. Initiate a meditation practice. Your intuition serves as your internal GPS, but you can only hear its guidance in the peaceful quiet. Find stillness, connect with the infinite part of yourself, and listen to your soul's whisperings.

Looking back on my journey, I am deeply grateful for the realization that my limitations were self-imposed. I now seek possibilities and embrace the new with open arms. I face challenges despite fear, taking each step with unwavering faith. I redefine my understanding of life success in a completely new way.

On the other side of my comfort zone, I discovered my purpose as a certified Life Coach. Having navigated major life transitions and embraced multiple pivots on my own journey, I possess the knowledge and tools to guide others through similar transformations. I am devoted to helping them navigate, pivot, and find the courage to create a life by design—one they never thought possible.

Go confidently in the direction of your dreams.
Live the life you have imagined.
~ Henry David Thoreau

About Elizabeth

Elizabeth Aguilera is a seasoned Life Mastery Consultant who possesses the expertise to guide individuals in designing and manifesting a life that aligns with their Soul's purpose. Having dedicated numerous years to studying and implementing transformational success principles, Elizabeth has become a highly sought-after speaker, teacher, and certified coach. Through her engaging workshops and coaching programs, she empowers people to shatter their limitations and accomplish extraordinary results.

Elizabeth's unwavering passion lies in educating her clients on unlocking their true potential, attaining extraordinary success, and creating a life they genuinely love. Having embarked on her own transformative journey, Elizabeth has crafted her second act as a certified Coach specializing in empowering women recovering from narcissistic abuse to heal, reclaim themselves, and create the vibrant life they deserve. Elizabeth serves as a guiding light, aiding clients to overcome self-doubt and empowering others to create a life by design, not by default!

Elizabeth's profound understanding of life's twists and turns stems from her extensive experience in the corporate world, where she worked as an IT professional for over three decades. When her position was outsourced to India, she fearlessly embarked on a successful entrepreneurial venture that catered to seniors and overwhelmed Moms, leaving her fully booked for a remarkable six years. Driven by an insatiable desire for personal growth, Elizabeth embarked on a transformative quest of self-discovery, uncovering her true essence and purpose. Applying the principles of transformational success to her own life, she propelled herself to the heights she had always aspired to reach.

Today, Elizabeth wholeheartedly embraces her empathic nature and follows her innate calling as a natural-born Coach, Teacher, Encourager, and Flourisher. If you yearn to gain clarity, confidence, and unlock your next level of success while experiencing profound fulfillment in all areas of your life, Elizabeth Aguilera's coaching programs are the transformative catalyst you need to get there.

In her leisure time, Elizabeth derives immense joy from singing in her church choir (mostly on key), volunteering within her local community, and lavishing attention on her sweet diva grandcat, Daisy.

Learn more at:

- https://elizabethaguilera.lifemasteryconsultant.com
- www.linkedin.com/in/elizabethaguilera
- www.facebook.com/thegoodcalling

CHAPTER 19

TRUST AND FALL INTO ALIGNMENT

BY MENA TEIJEIRO

'I don't want to be here anymore.'

This phrase was repeated over and over again, day after day, crowding hope out of my mind and weighing heavy on my heart. It was so strong that I shared it with close friends in an act of preservation. In a matter of a few weeks, I went from an emotional high just off a stage in Argentina giving my Tedx talk, to losing interest in being a part of this World.

During the short-lived celebration of the presentation, I received an anxious call telling me that someone very close to my family was sending the police to my nanny, accusing her of kidnapping my older son. What? This was insanity.

This caretaker who we loved and appreciated, had been coming to our home to support me with my boys for years. She had picked up my son from the dad's house earlier that day. Despite my efforts to explain the obvious, that it was my weekend and that she was given my authority to be with my son, the situation escalated. I had to change my airplane and rush back from Buenos Aires to Miami to pick up my boys.

As I was leaning into our parent coordinator meetings to understand what had happened and prevent it reoccurring, I was unexpectedly slapped in the face again. We had been divorced for six years and my life was anchored on being a mom and expanding my consciousness. I was told that the boys would be going to another school farther away, and that I would no longer have them all the weekdays and every other weekend; it would be a 50/50 time share.

While I was processing these visceral emotions, my energy healer (who had been my constant guide over the phone for the past two years) told me he wouldn't be able to continue supporting me. His girlfriend was jealous and didn't want him to facilitate sessions for me.

'I don't want to be here anymore!'

It had already been seven years since my awakening. I had realized that I had everything on the 'check-list' this society celebrates, and yet I felt that I wasn't a protagonist in my own life. I had married my first boyfriend, and we had two toddlers we both adored; he had moved us to Miami even though I had expressed clearly and repeatedly that I did not want to live there. A few months later, he went to work in Connecticut, leaving us back in Florida and coming to visit on weekends.

The determination to get divorced was fueled by a pulsating desire to live a life that was authentic and connected. The intention I set was clear; it took me on a thrill ride to shed my limitations, gain the courage of a lioness, and reinvent myself.

I devoted myself fully to healing for many years, transcending fear of public speaking, an eating disorder, emotional abuse, extreme sensitivity to energies, low self-esteem, divorce, chronic pain, multiple international and domestic relocations, single parenting, career transitions, and poor boundaries.

I had embarked on a lifelong process of self-discovery, studying from diverse teachers, traveling to mystical destinations, experiencing a multitude of different practices, publishing a book of poetry, getting many certifications for healing, movement, sound and consciousness, creating my own signature program, and guiding clients.

In spite of all that progress, at this moment, I felt like I was the ashes instead of the rising phoenix. I was trapped between not wanting to live and having to be here. My grandfather had acted upon this phrase before I was born and seeing how it had impacted my family's life so profoundly, I could not allow myself to come close to consider doing that to them.

I felt overwhelmed with my state of mind and I pushed through that week dancing at Art Basel events and trying to lift myself up. A friend encouraged me to make a bucket list that I could look forward to. Jumping off a plane was something I hadn't done before having my kids, and I had decided that it was not worth the risk of them losing their mom. That day, it had become the number one challenge on my list. Life is full of paradoxes.

The Universe heard me, as it is always listening, and at my insistence, graciously presented me with a way out. At an intersection, in the colorful Wynwood neighborhood in Miami, I was literally at a crossroads. Suddenly, I looked to my left and I could see the large 'SCHOOL BUS' words racing towards me. I linked eyes with the driver for eternity.

In that miraculous moment, I could have hit the brakes and my wish would have been granted. Instead, I looked at the other side of the road and I immediately accelerated out of the way…untouched. Just half a block later, I made it to my destination and parked my car. The message landed: My soul rushed me to safety! It chose to stay here on Earth. I didn't want to be here for the old way of living.

On January 11, 2018, I jumped out of a plane in Homestead, FL. It was a decision and a commitment to land on Earth with a big YES; to be here so fully, and to activate the life that my soul came for.

It was a trust fall…I rode on that one way flight with deep peace. "I am raising my hand, Universe! I'm here to live in alignment with creation. Support me, guide me. I choose to be a beacon of light." I landed like a lightning bolt; determined to be the brightest version of me in the midst of darkness.

My courage increased and I started to show up more and more to life. It was at this time that this question became a mantra in my life: 'How is this a gift?' Simply having this perspective unravels the blessings.

The sky would provide the next pivotal moment in my life. Hurricane Dorian (derived from the Greek word doron, meaning 'gift') blew in during September of 2019 to shake things up. This massive Category 5 hurricane parked over Bahamas, just a sneeze away from us. I had two multi-family investment properties in Miami that were supporting me financially, and I did not have hurricane insurance to protect my assets.

As we were driving up the east coast to avoid the storm, I connected with my massage therapist. I mentioned my concern and he expressed that he wished that his close friends, who were starting a mystery school, didn't live where they were. I needed to diversify and I verbalized that maybe I could invest in something that supported them too.

The next day, the couple shared a YouTube video of a property in Georgia that had iconic domes and was immersed in a lush forest with creeks. I was immediately hypnotized by its beauty, by the sale price (which was similar to one of my investment properties in Miami) and by the 182 acres... the numbers 8 and 2 combined were very dear to me; signifying infinity and duality. I reached out to the realtor!

Ten days later, I woke up earlier to send my boys off to school and be ready for my adventure. I took the first flight to Atlanta with my friend, rented a car, drove 90 minutes, and arrived at the location. As we drove through the half mile driveway and pulled up to the domes, my heart expanded and it whispered 'yes' to me again and again.

I was attentively hiking in my 'barefoot' shoes through the wild forest and I remember getting closer to the realtor for the moment of truth. I told him that I wouldn't get another real estate agent; he was the man who knew the seller's intentions; it had been on the market for two years at this point.

During the past decade, I had gained experience in the real estate world and had done relatively well with it. I learned to trust my instinct and meditate on the price. "If this property is meant for me, we will align with these numbers. If it's not meant to be, it's ok." I added. After, less than an hour at the property, we left so I could make it back to Miami in time to get my boys.

Days later, I heard back from the realtor with a contract! I was inspired to see that they accepted the number in the middle of my range and hadn't pushed for the highest. While I was under contract, I still needed to figure out how I was going to get a return on this investment. During a meeting to assess the validity of this project, the couple told me they had no way to pay me a rental for it. Even though I have a Booth MBA, I must admit that my decision was based on my gut feeling.

The closing date was moved to my dad's birthday, providing additional peace and validation to my heart. This was a clear message to my consciousness that I was supported by the divine masculine in my life. This time, the jump landed me on my own piece of heaven, The Florrest. What I did not anticipate was the amount of internal and external purging and growth I would still need to take on to make it my sacred sanctuary.

In February of 2020, there was an early stumble. I asked my massage therapist friend not to move there, to just visit for events, and he laughed at me with arrogance. "Why do you think you can make that decision?" I replied that I was the owner. He scoffed at me and then went to speak with his friends.

The people who had moved into the property didn't align with my requests for more transparency and communication. After expressing to me that I had broken the biblical timeline, they decided to leave. I made a quick day trip to talk to them face-to-face at the property and the man didn't come downstairs to meet me. He had never given me his cell phone either. I offered to pay them the management fee I had recently mentioned, and they declined it.

I am very grateful that they were a part of aligning with the property and that ultimately, we had a clean break. I learned that I need to claim what is mine with confidence, set clear boundaries, and be very specific about my intentions and agreements with others.

Soon after, quarantine began. Life was confined to being with my 11 and 13 years old boys in our apartment in Brickell, disinfecting supermarket deliveries, quick meals with long kitchen prep, and sitting through zoom calls.

When summer arrived, we freed ourselves in the forest, for what I initially thought would be a month. I fell in love with who I am in nature, sharing with friends and family, and taking action to make the property Airbnb ready.

My boys saw me blossom and bravely spoke up. "If you move here, we are going to live with dad!" For the past two years, their dad had been asking to have them live with him, and had promised to make it easy for me to visit. They had always been city boys, as I had been, and I understood that this was too isolated for them. I agreed to make that call…I simply opened my hands and off they went.

When I chose the yes in my heart, my 'nest' became empty seven years earlier than expected. Being away from my boys, who had been the center of my life since they were born, was crushingly difficult; I was locked out of their daily lives, told I wasn't a co-parent, and wasn't welcome into their home. There were no peaceful conversations or collaboration possible.

It was debilitating for me to feel that I had somehow lost my children. Eventually, I learned that nothing could stand between us. I could simply focus on enjoying the time I did have with them and making my days away from them valuable and vibrant to heal my heart, and harness the enthusiasm to keep going.

Soon after moving to Georgia, I started dating a man, who would become my best friend and partner for several years. He cocooned with me at The Florrest while he was going through his own raging divorce. I hired him and many others to help me develop the property (clean up eight containers full of yard trash, develop the amenities, and open 12 miles of trails). I felt supported as my vision unraveled.

For a while, there was no viable internet connection and the property was mostly in conservation; this meant I couldn't't promote it without severe fines. I learned to be quiet and work diligently; I burned all my bridges by investing all my resources and heart into this space. Why? I chose to claim the miracle; to mirror the oracle/truth that we are a spark of the divine! As source, we can magnetize all the authentic resources required for the life our soul came for.

When I exhaled, the conservation contract was over, rural broadband internet became available. I had created the infrastructure to host retreats, and guests were having magical experiences. Then, all my family came over during the summer for a retreat...it was a peak celebration for my soul to see them enjoy it; they could now experience what my heart trusted. In nature, we all belong, and find common ground no matter what our backgrounds are.

Having travelled extensively around the world gave me the maturity to commit to stewarding a forest. Retreats were my happy place, and with a thirst for transformation and development, I activated my gifts for creating sacred space for powerful awakening. From my own healing journey, I developed deep compassion for the shadows and trauma we experience as humans and a desire to celebrate our true nature.

My heart broke so many times that I know how to let go and be anchored in my center. I can profoundly connect and see others soar back to their lives. My own co-parenting struggles made me aware to create a business where I won't be crowded out of my manifestation.

I have integrated my passion for transformation and retreats, my intuitive gifts, my love for nature, and my work. Now, I jump in celebration that I have created an organic life where I am fully responsible for my environment, can blossom from my fertile foundation, guide others to live their authentic life, and collaborate with beautiful souls to ripple light into the World.

Life still presents challenges. Yet, as I continue to say yes to my inner knowing, I alchemize discomfort and the growth leads me to evolving alignment and fulfilment.

Trust. When you fall, choose to powerfully land on Earth!

About Mena

Mena Teijeiro is a possibilities igniter – a hybrid of the world of business and the realm of conscious exploration. She found common ground in nature where she offers sacred space for profound transformation. Mena guides heart-centered souls to create a fertile foundation for their lives to scale in a sustainable and authentic way.

Born in Argentina in 1977, she grew up in a loving family with four siblings and her two parents. Early on, she experienced cultural diversity and uprooting when moving to DC between the ages of five and ten and traveling around the world with her family for extended holidays. Early on, she learned how to be inclusive and welcoming with all people. Her life had the abundance of community, resources, education, and opportunities, yet lacked the emotional guidance to love herself and trust her inner voice.

Mena dedicated herself to doing her best in all areas of life; economist, COO of an internet startup, intern in DC at the IIF. She worked with investment bankers in Chicago and Buenos Aires, became a wife, a Booth MBA (multi-lingual), was on the business recovery team at PwC in London, and then was a full-time mom for her two wonderful boys.

A multi-passionate soul (intellectually and physically), she was strongly influenced by her environment and outwardly thrived. Within, she had many wounds and insecurities…she had failed herself by ignoring her inner landscape and not knowing how to set boundaries.

In 2010, Mena got divorced and went off the beaten path into higher dimensions to start creating a life that felt like home. Now, she is a highly intuitive consultant (certified in many modalities) supporting souls to return to their sovereign power. She is the managing owner of The Florrest (retreat center nestled in 153 acres of forest in middle Georgia), creator of Awaken Flow™ framework, a TEDx speaker, and the author of *The Alchemy of Words, Poems of Truth to Transform your Inner Landscape.*

Mena values authenticity, collaboration, and an organic approach to life. You will find her playing in her forest, clearing a trail, creating her next project, visiting or traveling with her boys, learning a new modality or skill, and collaborating with souls who appreciate and encourage each other to bring more light into our beloved planet.

Her greatest achievement will always be trusting her intuition, aligning with her fulfilment, and being a source of joy and guidance for those who want to receive their divine inheritance. It's contagious, so if you are interested, find out what she's up to at:

- www.menafesting.com

CHAPTER 20

THE FOUR ELEMENTS OF SUCCESS

BY PAUL PETERS

Introduction

Success is measured differently by many people. For some, it's to obtain possessions or wealth, for others it is achieving a major goal, and for yet others, it is reaching some spiritual pinnacle. Here, I will redefine success and provide readers some practical tips on how to achieve their goals and meet their own definition of a successful life.

It is important to:

1) Set clear and specific goals in order to meet your definition of success.
2) Break down large goals into smaller, more manageable ones.
3) Create a plan of action to achieve them.

Additionally, the significance of taking responsibility for one's own life and not relying on external factors or other people to determine one's success cannot be stressed enough.

One of the key takeaways from this book is that success is not just about achieving material wealth or status – which might be an outcome or by-product of your pursuit. It's about finding fulfillment in all areas of life, including relationships, health, and personal growth. I encourage readers to define their own version of success and work towards it on their own terms, but with a clear plan on how to do that.

Achieving your goals is a journey that requires determination, hard work, and perseverance. However, it is important to remember that the journey to achieving your goals should be on your own terms. This means that you should not allow external factors such as societal expectations or peer pressure to dictate how you pursue your dreams.

To achieve your goals on your own terms, it requires four key elements that can be used for whatever dream you have:

First:

It is essential to have a clear understanding of what you want to accomplish; you must have a vision or picture of what you want. Call this your ultimate destination. It must be so clear in your mind's eye that you can see it, smell it, and feel it as if you are experiencing it presently. It starts with a clear and focused vision of what you want by placing it in your mind. You should have the picture in your mind – just as an architect has a finished model of the completed building prior to any work being done.

Second:

You must identify why this is important to you and it must be connected to your purpose – which is what awakens your soul's desire. It's important that it be connected to your purpose because out of your purpose (what you are to do that you are best at), comes the best of who you are. This may often be referred to as your 'unique ability' or your gift. Once you have identified your vision and it is connected to your purpose, you must now walk out and head in the direction of your vision.

Action is key to fulfillment of your goal, much like a driver enters this destination into his GPS system. The GPS then breaks down and shows the steps how to get there. For us, this involves setting specific and measurable goals that align with our purpose. It also requires developing a plan of action that outlines the steps you need to take, to achieve these goals. With your Vision and your sense of purpose you then move to the third element.

Third:

The third element is your passion. Along the way, there will be obstacles and challenges that may test your resolve. However, staying true to yourself and maintaining focus and passion on what matters most to you will help you overcome these hurdles. It is highly recommended you surround yourself with positive mentors and coaches who can encourage you and support you. You must also continue to fuel your purpose with the passion that will carry you through your challenges.

Your passion is your source of power that enables you to do that which you never thought possible. It was Martin Luther King's passion that fueled his mission for equal rights for blacks. It was Mother Teresa's passion for the downtrodden and homeless that changed the world's heart towards the less fortunate. Our passion is what gets us across the finish line in our pursuit of success.

It is also important to celebrate small victories along the way as they serve as motivation for continued progress towards achieving larger milestones, as well as to always have a grateful and thankful spirit. A grateful and thankful spirit takes us out of fear and doubt into the realm of acceptance of what we haven't yet obtained, but know we possess.

The very 'Knowing' ushers in the outcome most desired. The 'Knowing' process consists of three parts: (a) it starts with a dream, want and goal created out of the imagination of the mind that entails thinking clearly what you want; (b) it requires the powerful element of faith or belief in your dream without question; and (c) it means living out that dream, want and goal as if you already possess it and you are experiencing those feelings now in the present.

Finally:

The fourth element is love. Achieving your goals on your own terms requires self-awareness, determination, resilience and most importantly love. Love is the greatest attribute we must give to ourselves and others. When we have a vision, and connect it to our purpose, fueled by passion and motivated or driven by love, then success is guaranteed. By staying true to yourself and focusing on what matters most, you can create a fulfilling journey towards accomplishing your dreams.

Overall, there are valuable insights into achieving success in all aspects of life by setting clear goals and taking responsibility for one's actions, while defining success on one's own terms. In order to illustrate the process, let me introduce you to a man named Tim. Tim found success in growing through his struggles to find his calling, purpose, and life – after facing many challenges. Tim's story is a familiar one for most of us who aren't given the roadmap to success, and through the trials of life, he must figure it out on his own terms.

***

TIM'S STORY

Tim's childhood was fraught with challenges for a young kid. His mom, a mother of six, was a victim of domestic violence at the hands of her husband, Tim's alcoholic father. His mom was forced to be on the run with her six kids due to abuse. His father eventually was sentenced to prison for the attempted murder of Tim's mother when she was hospitalized for a year from gunshot wounds to her abdomen. His mother eventually recovered and remarried, and although Tim desired a loving relationship from a father figure, it was never to be found in his new stepfather. Even though he never knew his real Dad and was never close to his stepfather, Tim was close to his mother, She always believed in him and encouraged him to pursue his dreams.

Tim's life had been marked by various challenges and painful experiences. From a young age, he sought to escape his difficult home life by immersing himself in work, sex and alcohol. Tim's propensity for lying and his desire for acceptance led him down a destructive path of alcohol abuse, unhealthy relationships, and self-destructive behavior.

Despite the difficulties he faced, Tim managed to graduate from high school while struggling academically due to drug and alcohol issues. He was able to get into college, but still struggled with his addictions and resentment towards his now-deceased Father. Tim's experiences growing up in a turbulent environment, witnessing and experiencing abuse, and struggling to find his place in the world, shaped his perspective on life.

During his college years, Tim faced a career-ending injury, struggled with low grades, and went through multiple breakups with his on-and-off girlfriends. He sought refuge in alcohol and engaged in promiscuous behavior, further exacerbating his pain and creating a cycle of self-destruction. Tim's life took a dark turn when he experienced a psychological breakdown and engaged in self-harm while intoxicated. Although this event scared him, he continued to numb his pain with alcohol and destructive relationships.

Tim's life continued on a downward spiral as he lost his job, apartment, and car, leaving him homeless and desperate. He contemplated suicide, but was interrupted by a clear inner voice that urged him to stop. This experience led him to believe that God was speaking to him, offering him hope and a chance at life again.

He reached out to his brother for help and began to recognize the destructive consequences of his choices. He slowly began to rebuild his life. He realized that the choices he had made, as well as the choices made by others that affected him, had led him away from the path he was meant to follow. Tim's journey serves as a reminder of the consequences of unresolved issues and the transformative power of faith and second chances. Tim's life took a complete turn when he decided to abstain from alcohol and sex and dedicated himself to volunteering at the church. He became heavily involved in various ministries, found a sense of purpose, and experienced joy and peace for the first time in his life. Through his involvement in the church and volunteering at the local non-profit, Tim discovered his passion for helping others who were struggling with addiction and emotional issues.

Tim's story highlights the early years of his life – marked by adversity, resilience, and personal growth. It sets the stage for the subsequent chapters in Tim's life, where Tim's journey continued as he navigated through relationships, education, and his pursuit of a career in counseling. He realized the importance of empathy, understanding, and the power of resilience. These realizations planted the seeds for his future career as a counselor, where he would be able to support and guide others facing similar challenges.

During this time, Tim also addressed the root of his pain, which stemmed from his strained relationship with his father. He learned to forgive his father and release the anger and hate he had held onto for so many years. This forgiveness brought him freedom and healing, and he recognized that God could provide the love and acceptance he had always longed for. As Tim began to heal from the emotional wounds that affected every aspect of his life, he was able to use that healing to help others heal, and, in a sense, have a deeper understanding of why he went through the pain.

As Tim's journey continued, he understood that his past did not define him and he embraced the healing and transformation God had brought into his life. He recognized the importance of addressing wounded souls and finding acceptance and love in healthy ways. Tim's purpose and calling continued to unfold, and he understood that self-discovery and discovering God were intertwined. He saw how God used his suffering and mistakes to shape him and help him grow. Tim's journey was a testament to the power of forgiveness, healing, and finding purpose through serving others.

Although Tim started with challenges, he took those challenges and made them his strengths, discovering his vision, his purpose, his passion and ultimately, his love in serving others to redefine success in his own terms.

CONCLUSION

As we reflect on Tim's journey to discover success, we must look at how these four elements of success are part of that roadmap for all of us. For myself, serving those with disabilities through my company and with my non-profit, I am able to help many less-fortunate folks. They can begin to dream and, through the use of those four elements, they are provided a pathway for them to reach their goals.

I am working on directing others to seek after their dreams by helping them identify their gifts, talents, strengths, and passions, and then put them to work in an area of the company where they will use these gifts to thrive and prosper. If I am doing something I love and I am called to do it, I will be successful. Success Redefined for me is about following my purpose fueled by my passion to love and serve others.

Over the last two years, the outworking of that was the formulation of the non-profit – 'The Nehemiah Project Covenant of Love.' This idea came out of much prayer and study in the book of Nehemiah. Nehemiah (a Jew) was a cup-bearer to King Artaxerxes, King of Persia around 444 BC. His home city of Jerusalem was in ruin after the destruction of the wall by their enemies. The Jews had just been released from captivity and Nehemiah was sorrowful over the condition of his home. His master saw his sorrow and asked how he could help. He asked that he be allowed to return and assist in rebuilding the wall to help restore and rebuild the city. The King allowed him to do so and paid for the venture. Working through great difficulties from their enemies, Nehemiah and other Jews restored the wall and the city to its former glory, and brought revival to the people. There were six towers in Jerusalem that had to be restored.

God revealed to me the amazing symbolism and significance in the current condition in our communities. He helped me see that different towers represent areas of our society that are broken and need to be restored and healed. Those areas include seniors, veterans, those struggling with addiction, the intellectually disabled, those with mental health issues, the homeless, at-risk kids and abused mothers. My response was to follow my dream which came to be called 'The Nehemiah Project' – which was formulated as a non-profit to begin serving these towers. I started first in Stanly County, and ultimately it spread throughout the whole state of North Carolina.

Rather than only work directly with the one church we had chosen to work with, we encouraged the church as well as all other community partners that have a heart for those in each of the towers to come together to bring healing and help restore the community – as Nehemiah did in his time. I came to recognize that it first starts with a heart's desire to serve and love others, then a compassionate heart to want to do something about it, then an obedient heart to go and do the work. But, most importantly, you need a humble heart to allow God to help you in the process.

With a mission to come alongside those who suffer and provide love, support, mentoring, and service, the organization aims to bring hope and a sense of purpose to individuals within their community. By working with both the church and other community partners, we seek to unite people in like acts of service that will lead to healing and to the rebuilding of the community.

My own journey of finding my vision, purpose, passion and love in service, emphasizes the importance of a heart's desire to serve, a compassionate heart to act, an obedient heart to do the work, and a humble heart to allow God's guidance throughout the process. My hope is that these four elements will be your tools to guide you in first identifying what success is for you. Then, it should give you the direction to go after them to achieve and live out your dreams.

There is a particular passage that best relates to me on this subject
out of Jeremiah 29:11:
For I know the plans I have for you declares the Lord,
plans to prosper you, and not to harm you,
plans to give you hope and a future.

About Paul

Paul Peters was born in Carbondale, Illinois to George and Dolores Peters. He was raised in the suburbs of Chicago and attended Homewood Flossmoor High School where he was involved in Gymnastics. Paul graduated from the University of Illinois with a bachelor's in Psychology. He then attended Seminary where he studied Philosophy at Southern Evangelical Seminary and served as a chaplain in the New York jail system. He had the honor of serving in the Army for eight years and received an honorable discharge as a First Lieutenant.

Paul has three amazing children who mean the world to him; his daughter is in college at Clemson, his youngest son graduated with a double degree from the University of South Carolina, and his eldest son remains at home with a caregiver who cares for him. Paul is the proud owner of Covenant Case Management Services which is a service organization that serves individuals with disabilities in North Carolina. He is also the founder of 'The Nehemiah Project Covenant of Love', a non-profit that serves and supports the following areas: homelessness, veterans, senior citizens, those struggling with addiction, those with mental health issues, substance abuse, developmental disabilities, at-risk kids and abused women in the state of North Carolina.

Paul started a Mentoring Center in 2022 under the Nehemiah Project that seeks to make a positive impact for at-risk kids. He is a published author of two books, *Discovering and Embracing Your Life Purpose*, and *The Ways of Wisdom*, and is currently working on his third book – *Success Redefined*, with Jack Canfield.

Paul's passions are reading, being the best version of himself, serving others, traveling, and helping people discover their purpose in life. He is all about living life to the fullest each day and having a positive influence on all those he meets.

CHAPTER 21

MY NINE KEYS TO SUCCESS

BY ROBERT LOUIS CRANE

Failure Is the Road to Success. I have not failed.
I've just found 10,000 ways that won't work.
~ Thomas Edison

Key #1:

It is not What Happens To You that determines The Quality Of Your Life.
It is What You Do About It.
~ Tony Robbins

My father Earl got knocked down four times by life events but he got back up five. He has been a lifelong inspiration to my determination to succeed. My mother Marie always reminded us that, "We come from good stock."

1. My father Earl Crane was a radio operator on a B-24 Bomber in WWII. He was shot down February 24th, 1944, on his 15th mission taking part in 'Big Week' a week of concentrated attacks on the German aircraft industries. His pilot, James O McMullin Jr., gave the ultimate sacrifice by going down with the plane saving his 9 other crew members. Earl, wounded by shrapnel, was left hanging by his parachute in a tree with a broken collar bone. He survived 14 months in a German Prison Camp. Earl met and fell in love with my mother Marie Schoendienst in 1943 before he shipped out. They met at a USO dance. After liberation, they were happily married for 53 years and raised seven boys and one girl. Earl started the Crane Roofing and Siding business.

I wrote and dedicated these two songs to my father and Lt. McMullen:

- All I Ever Wanted
- We Fly The Flag

2. Sometime later, Earl was falsely diagnosed with Tuberculosis. He was forced to spend six months in hospital isolation with no income or direct family contact allowed. He had Pleurisy and not TB. After being released, he once again started up Crane Roofing.

3. Weakened from his prolonged hospitalization, Earl fell off a ladder onto a metal staple gun while roofing and crushed his pelvis, destroying his ball-and-socket joint. They fused his thigh bone to his hip, and he spent six months in a body cast at home. Crane Roofing would never re-open. Earl got retrained as a machinist for The Continental Can Company.

4. Continental Can fired Earl one year short of his 20th year which would have qualified him for a pension.

January 1991 – A record $415 million settlement was won against the Continental Can Co. proving that Earl and some 3,000 other employees were targeted for layoffs to avoid having to pay their pensions. Continental Can used a scheme known as the 'Bell' plan, a reverse acronym for 'Let's Limit Employee Benefits.' The sum is one of the largest ever in a case brought under the Employee Retirement Income Security Act. Earl did not live to see his portion of the settlement. It was awarded to my mother who survived him by 12 years.

Key#2 - *Employ The Powerful Laws of Attraction*

Imagination is everything. It is the preview of life's coming attractions.
~ Albert Einstein

1973 – At age 15 in Florida, I wrote down my goal to live and surf in Hawaii. I started reading *Surfer Magazine* adventure stories and hung a Hawaiian surfing poster on my wall and dreamed about living in Hawaii. While I was in high school, I paid for 40 hours of private pilot lessons with my earnings as drywall hanger. After graduating, I enrolled in commercial pilot school and secured a student loan to start college in January 1976. One morning before work I read a want ad that *forever changed my life*: 'Wanted – Lifeguard with sales experience' – Pool Boys International. I cancelled pilot school and took that independent contractor's offer running hotel pool and beach concessions because they said one day they would expand to Hawaii.

March 25th, 1977, age 19 – After stints in Florida, Las Vegas, and San Diego hotels with Pool Boys, I paddled out and rode my first wave at Waikiki Beach. I was a Pool Boys concessionaire at the Hilton Hawaiian Village Resort realizing my dream of living and surfing in Hawaii! I focused on my goal, believed and took action.

Key #3 – *Trust Your Gut*

September 1977 – After six months in Waikiki, Pool Boys offered me the new Kauai Island concession at the Kauai Surf Hotel. Six months later they closed the Kauai concession and asked me to go back to California. I declined and submitted a proposal to the resort, and they awarded me the contract for the concession. At age 20, I started my first corporation in Hawaii called Island Adventure Inc.

In 1978, the hotel manager, his doctor friend and I started the Kauai River Adventure on the Huleia River. I met Harrison Ford while they were filming *Raiders of The Lost Ark* on this river. The movie production paid us not to operate while they filmed Indiana's 'snake in the float plane' scene escaping the arrows and spears of the natives.

From 1979 –1981, we opened three other hotel concessions at the Sheraton Coconut Beach, Poipu Kai and Princeville Resorts and a second river tour with a hike to a waterfall. I was renting a 3-story beach house on Moloaa Bay. My brother Michael met the love of his life, his current wife Bonnie of 40 plus years after she went on our river tour. My gut and the Joy of surfing lead me to find my calling teaching water sports and entertaining people. Life was fantastic!

Key #4 – The Gift of Conflict

Always look for the Gift of Conflict
~ Positive Intelligence (Shirzad Chamine)

November 23rd, 1982 – Hurricane Iwa hit Kauai. Iwa destroyed 2,345 buildings, including 1,927 houses, leaving 500 people homeless. Damage totaled $312 million. Many businesses closed permanently.

After Iwa, we lost our employees, the 4 hotel concessions and all we had invested in the past 5 years. We filed bankruptcy and started over. Turns out we were in good company as Henry Ford and Walt Disney had both filed for bankruptcy and went on to create the Model T, Ford Motors, Mickey Mouse and Disneyland. Incidentally, we paid back our local Hawaiian business vendors after the bankruptcy on Kauai by paying cash for new services while also paying back the bankrupted amounts.

My Life Changing Gift of Conflict

I stayed on Kauai after Iwa to rebuild. At age 26 in 1984, I met the love of my life, my future wife Mary Jennings. She was working at La Luna, the only Mexican restaurant on Kauai. February 2nd, 2024, marks 40 years together. The conflict of the hurricane brought Mary to me the best gift I have ever received.

Key #5 – *If You Don't Know Why Something Can't Be Done You Just Might Succeed At Doing It.*

My mother Marie would do whatever others told her she couldn't. I believed we could rebuild our business though many did not. In 1987, five years after Hurricane Iwa, another unwanted visitor came to Kauai. The IRS knocked on my kayak shack door. A chill went up my spine. The agent said we were delinquent on back taxes. He explained that many businesses on Kauai were also delinquent due to the hurricane. His job was to get us in compliance or close us down. He set us up on a payment plan. The money we owed for back taxes had been spent keeping the business alive for the past five years. This critical time allowed Kauai tourism to rebound just enough for us to return to profitability. *Not knowing the tax consequences beforehand saved our business.*

Key #6 – *Know Your Why And Your What And How Will Follow.*

Lightning struck twice in the same place when the second hurricane Iniki slammed into Kauai September 5th, 1992: Iniki killed six people causing $3 billion in damage, destroying 1,400 homes and damaging 13,000 more. Steven Spielberg was filming *Jurassic Park* on Kauai when Iniki made landfall. We survived two hurricanes in ten years but lost everything we had worked for, twice. We struggled four years to rebuild the business. We sold it in 1996 for only $50,000, just a fraction of what it was worth.

<u>My Why</u> – We decided to find another line of work impervious to hurricanes. Mary and I moved to the San Francisco Bay Area where she was raised. I was offered a sales job with a tax firm. This firms' specialty was of all things, representing businesses and individuals with IRS and state tax problems. Ironically, my ten years of post-hurricane business survival made me the 'poster boy' for the type of clients they helped. My business struggles had been my 'on the job training for my next career.' God certainly has a great sense of humor! My why was to help others with transformational tax solutions. Taxes are impervious to hurricanes.

<u>My What and How</u> – I met John Bove, a licensed Enrolled Agent, while working in that tax firm. John and I went on to open our own IRS and State tax representation firm Ameritax LLC on December 7th, 1997. We started on a shoestring budget incubating in a larger CPA firm, and we built the business to over a million in revenues by 2007 with 10 employees. We have been working together for over 25 years.

Key #7 – Never Stop Learning About Your Business

You Don't Learn Less. Not Getting It Is What Takes All The Time.
~ Money and You workshops (Marshal Thurber)

The subprime mortgage crisis was a business storm that caused $7.4 trillion in stock market paper losses and wiped out about $3.4 billion in real estate wealth. Many companies went bankrupt, and about 7.5 million Americans lost jobs, with the unemployment rate doubling to 10% in 2010. This severe economic recession caused our company Ameritax to lose hundreds of thousands of dollars in client receivables.

Welcome to the 'Learning Team'

<u>Our First Mistake</u> – We financed our client's fees with an affordable 'something down and something a month' plan. When the recession occurred 90% of our clients could not pay us for the work we had completed.

<u>Our Second Mistake</u> – We unwittingly employed the *'diving board method of marketing.'* We had one 3-meter board over one segment of the marketing pool called Google Pay Per Click. The recession drained that pool, and we were left with only 25% of our annual sales. This ended our phenomenal run of quadrupling sales in 2005 to 2008 from $250k to over 1 million in revenue. We could not pay our bills including more taxes and I filed my 2nd business bankruptcy in 2010 and nearly lost my home. Many much larger firms like Lehman Brothers, the New York-based investment bank with assets worth 691 billion U.S. dollars also filed bankruptcy.

Key #8 – *Do What Brings You Joy And Happiness And Success Will Find You.*

Have the courage to follow your heart and intuition. They somehow already know what you truly want to become. Everything else is secondary.
~ Steve Jobs

I love to teach. I especially love it when what I teach transforms someone's life for the better. Every day I am blessed to get do the work which I en-JOY. I love it when a client breaks down with tears of relief after they realize that they are not alone. They begin to for the first time, let go of the fear and shame they often have carried for years. A huge burden gets lifted, and a ray of hope starts to shine on them as we educate them about all their tax solution options. I know firsthand from my hurricane days what it feels like to go it alone and try to navigate the collection systems of the IRS and state tax authorities.

We provide a sort of 'Financial Therapy' as they learn about what is possible with our top ten tax solutions approach. They are:

1. Pay in Full,
2. Pay monthly installments.
3. Qualify for a non-collectable status due to financial hardship.
4. Make an Offer In Compromise and settle for less than owed.
5. Wait out the IRS 10-year collection statute expiration dates.
6. File a bankruptcy on the income taxes
7. Do Nothing–often used before people hire us.
8. Prove you do not owe.
9. Apply for innocent spouse remedies.
10. Apply for penalty abatement.

I often forget what time it is in my daily work with clients. I look up and 10 hours have gone by in a wink. The work I enjoy comes with the word joy built right into it.

Key #9 – *Find A Way to Leave People in a Better Place Than You Found Them*

<u>Transformational Tax Solution Stories</u>

Stephen King might like some of our clients' real-life horror stories for his movies. Most of our client's tax problems are caused by unexpected severe life events, like cancer, natural disasters, divorce, business failures, life-changing accidents and injuries and family deaths of the breadwinners. We have developed a unique form of 'financial therapy' that fosters life-changing transformation for our clients. Here are just a few of those stories.

We release IRS and State wage and bank levies. A client was referred to us with both his paycheck and bank account levied by the IRS and the State. He assumed that he would lose his job, then his house and would not be able to provide for his teenage daughter. He had become depressed and despondent. We filed his missing returns allowing the release of the levies in 72 hours. This protected his living expenses as we set up an affordable payment plan.

Another client inherited her deceased sister's home. She discovered thousands of dollars in tax liens on the property. We proved there was identity theft and fraudulent tax returns filed using her stolen information. We got the liens removed.

The IRS assessed another client over $26.7 million. He was a day trader for years with thousands of small stock trades. We prepared his missing returns and then settled the debt with the IRS Offer in Compromise Program for $40,000.

One other client called and was panicked about receiving an IRS wage levy for over $265,000 – taking a large portion of her paycheck for several weeks. Our research revealed she had inherited a home from her deceased husband and sold it. The tax return had been improperly prepared and did not allocate her stepped up basis which would have shown no capital gain tax was due. We corrected the turn, got the IRS wage levy released the same day and the IRS had to refund the levied wages back to her. She simply did not owe the tax.

We have thousands of client success stories. We love helping people to transform their tragedies into solutions. For over 25 years we have implemented life-changing transformational tax solutions that restore the hope and dreams of our clients. My *Nine Keys to Success* unlocked my potential.

About Robert

A business owner for over 40 years with experience in Hawaii tourism and a nationwide tax firm, Robert Crane now provides life-transforming solutions for his tax clients.

Bob lived in Hawaii for 14 years and loved to surf, sail and scuba dive. He started the first ever Kayak River Tour in Hawaii back in 1977. His tours operated for over 18 years and were featured on travel adventure shows like *PM Magazine*. Stories from travel writers about his tours were featured in many magazines like *Cosmopolitan* and *Life* when he hosted the cast of the 1993 miniseries *The Thorn Birds*, with Richard Chamberlain, Rachael Ward and Brian Brown on the Kalihiwai River Adventure. His tours were featured in major tour operator programs like American Express Travel, Pleasant Hawaiian Holidays and American Hawaii Cruises. Bob ran hotel pool and beach concessions on Kauai for Sheraton Coconut Beach, Kauai Surf Resort, and activities booking centers at Poipu Kai and Princeville resorts. He guided adventure sea kayaking and camping trips on the Nāpali Coast on Kauai, the North Coast of Molokai, Tahiti, Samoa, and the Cook Islands.

Since Hawaii, Bob has spent the past 25 years in the tax industry where he is recognized as a leading expert in tax resolution solutions. His ability to take the stress out of the process for his clients and simplify the complex IRS and State procedures makes him unique in the mostly fear-driven industry. As President of Fix Your Tax Problem Inc., Bob oversees client cases from all over the US and has successfully resolved thousands of client tax cases in all fifty states.

Bob is also a songwriter and musician and has written over 50 songs. For the past 12 years, Bob has been a voting member of the Recording Academy which selects the Grammy winners each year. He has been the San Rafael chapter manager of West Coast Songwriters, a nonprofit organization for 13 years. He runs a monthly song writing open mic to provide a place for songwriters to share their music. He is a 13-year member of Business Network International and has served as one of their director consultants for the past three years, helping other chapter members grow their businesses.

He and his wife Mary love their home in San Rafael where they have resided for 30 years. They met and fell in love on Kauai in 1984. They celebrate 40 years together on February 2nd, 2024.

For more info about Bob:

- www.fixyourtaxproblem.com
- www.robertcranemusic.com

For info on his father, Earl Crane, and his plane, missions and crew in WW II, visit:
- https://www.americanairmuseum.com/archive/aircraft/42-40733

CHAPTER 22

AVOIDING DÉJÀ VU

BY GAIL A. GRENZIG, PhD

I used to hate New Years. Now don't get me wrong, I enjoy a good party like anyone else, but New Year's Day brings new resolutions and reminders of things I wanted to accomplish last year but for whatever reason didn't. Time to lose weight once again! No more desserts, forget pizza, and the worst of all, prying open that overly stuffed, dreaded junk drawer and sorting through the abandoned assortment of 'stuff' to find my elusive gym membership card. Come on now, I bet you have one of those drawers too!

Picture this. The evening of January 1st I decide to get organized. Certainly, that is way to finally achieve my goal. I find the perfect water bottle and color coordinated shorts, top, and wrist bands, in case I sweat. Time to find the membership card! I bravely give the junk drawer a good tug and to my surprise it opens with little resistance. Let the scavenger hunt begin! I reached into the abyss and slowly pull out one shoelace, birthday cards from six months ago, keys to unfamiliar locks, adapters to unknown electronics, stacks of papers and store coupons. Naturally, I pause to reread each card, check coupon expiration dates, and try to recall what goes with what. Finally, towards the back of the drawer, I find the membership card! Victoriously, I take the stockpiled stuff on the counter and shove it back in the drawer; I can deal with that another day. It's time to get ready for the gym!

The alarm broke the dark silence of the early morning and frankly, broke my heart. 5:30 AM was way too early. Did I even sleep? Then I suddenly remembered, it was time. Time to rise and shine, time to get my head in the game, and time to be all that I could be. Victory was mine!

I crawled out of bed towards the kitchen and morning's black elixir, coffee. No more sugar and cream for me; nope, I would drink it black. It's not the same, but the calories. After drinking every medicinal drop, I headed out the door, started the car and my journey to the new me. "Haven't I done this before?" I asked myself. I knew I had, but this time was going to be different, I promised myself.

The gym was crowded, more crowded than I remembered from the last time I set foot in there over six months ago. I wondered why and recalled the same thing happened last year. All those people with resolutions returned to the gym on January 2nd. I approached the bicycles hoping to join a spin class, but they were all taken. Standing next to me was a small group of lean, muscular individuals who were grumbling about not being able to get their daily workout completed before work because of the 'resolutioners.' This group was the regulars, the frequent flyers who flocked to the gym ritualistically every morning. The sudden influx of 'wanna-be' gym rats swarmed each area of the gym likes bees to pollen, hoping the new routines would stick. I'm not a 'wanna-be' I thought to myself; I am actually going to do it this year. Hadn't I said that before?

As you can imagine, the story repeated as it had for every previous year. I started out strong, but slowly over time, I made excuses, rationalized my absence, and eventually reverted back to my previous ways and habits. The membership card ended up in the drawer with full abandonment. It was another déjà vu moment.

I believe I am a fairly well-educated, intelligent woman. But what I have come to learn is that intelligence has nothing to do with being SMART. Like many of you, I was that gerbil on a wheel constantly spinning, and getting nowhere. Only recently have I figured out how to stop the spinning, accomplish more goals, and turn my efforts into winning.

How did I do this? It's simple, but not easy. It first started with realizing that I had not really set attainable goals for myself; instead, I had ideals.

It is an ideal to lose weight, an ideal to find more life balance, an ideal to get healthy, and an ideal to change careers, for example. But these are not goals. Ideals are pictures of what we want to accomplish, but there is no actual road map on how to get there. Goals actually needs to be specific, observable, measurable, and within a defined timeframe. Ideals are non-specific and not measurable. For example, what does the ideal of losing weight really mean? ...5 pounds? ...50 pounds? The ideal doesn't state how or by when this will be accomplished. By design, ideals are vague enough to give us enough rope to hang ourselves. We are all doomed to fail because accountability is virtually non-existent.

Years ago, while watching the movie, *Philadelphia*, I was struck by a line Denzel Washington repeated frequently. He played an attorney and continuously asked others to explain their testimony as if he were a six-year-old. In other words, break it down to the most basic level. Author Robert Fulghum echoed this perspective stating that everything we needed to learn in life we learned in kindergarten. Organizational psychologist Adam Grant agreed, stating that everything we need to achieve our goals already lies within us. This sentiment resonated with me. Instead of looking outside, I needed to look within. It was simple; we all need to be six-year-olds, breaking ideals down to basic levels, creating achievable goals.

When I looked inside, I discovered that getting basic was a good start, but not enough. I also needed to get smarter. Getting smarter has nothing to do with intelligence. Getting smarter meant that I needed to develop a plan, a blueprint, or compass to help me succeed. Without this, I was lost, building a house of cards, ready to tumble with the slightest breeze. No, I needed a blueprint to establish a strong foundation upon which I could build. My blueprint came in the form of SMART goals. What exactly are SMART goals? They are goals that provide us with a specific structure to guide us to success. They are goals that are Specific, Measurable, Attainable, Relevant, and Time-bound (hence SMART). Let's drill down a bit into each of the areas to help the six-year-old inside of you understand.

Specific means that you define what you expect, who will do it, and outline accountability. For me, I expected to lose a total of 20 pounds, a minimum of one pound a week for 20 weeks. Accountability came in the form of my Apple watch to track my exercise requirements of 45 minutes a day, minimally five days a week. My exercise of choice was pickleball, swimming, or walking. Additionally, using an app I tracked my calories staying under 1200 at least five times per week. I weighed myself daily.

You might ask yourself, why am I using apps to track everything? Dominican University professor, Gail Matthews, determined that each of us is 42% more likely to complete a goal if we write it down. Why? Because it clarifies exactly what we are trying to accomplish, has built in accountability, and provides motivation to sustain the change process and achieve. For me, it was apps on my watch that I continually carried with me. Some of you may need the paper chart hung on the refrigerator or a notebook journal. For me, using the combination of my phone and watch worked well because the apps produced visible data and tracked my progress. On an aside, I also had the motivation of fitting into my dress for my son's upcoming wedding! No matter which way you choose to go, be sure it's visible and written down in a form that works for you. This is the optimal way to hold ourselves accountable.

Measurable is the next component of the SMART goal. This is the criteria, usually a numerical quantity, that determines success. It can be 25% response to a survey, writing a minimum of 350 words a day (my current criteria), one pound per week, two date nights per month, or whatever applies to you. Just make sure it is measurable kindergarten basic.

Attainable comes next. When we think about goals, we want to make sure that we have the time, resources, and authority to move forward. Sometimes there are factors beyond our control. We need to take this all into consideration. If my goal is to save $1,000 by the end of the year, achieving this by playing Powerball each month is not likely attainable. But if I decide to make my own coffee every day instead of buying it, I can save money and the probability of attaining my goal is high.

Relevance is the next SMART goal component. You are here right now, because there is something in your life you want to change, enhance, or simply do better. For some, it could even be finding greater life balance and success. Relevance is the determinant of your personal 'why.' Only you can answer the question of why now, but it is an important question to answer with specificity. I encourage you to take a few moments right now to think and write about your why. It is important to know why you want to change.

Time is the final component, but one that has a double-edge. Strictly speaking, when creating our SMART goal, we need to specify when the goal should be completed. We specify the exact date in terms of days, weeks, or years. This adds the final dimension to accountability. We either succeed or fail based upon the criteria of time, it's that simple.

But the concept of time has duality that can be either an objective or obstacle. Time establishes accountability, but it can also be an excuse. I was the master of excuses. I didn't have enough time to go to the gym or not enough time to devote to my writing. I used time as my way out.

There is a significant misnomer in our world about the concept of time management. Let me state this clearly; there is no such thing as time management. It simply doesn't exit. This is because time has no true physical state. Think of it like an ocean wave. If you dip your hand into the ocean, you quickly realize that you can't hold onto the wave. It slips through your fingers and continues to move forward. The same holds true for time.

If we can't manage time, what can we manage? Ourselves. We can track the time we spend on what. We can use apps, charts, or journals to determine how we decide to use the resource of time. This was my starting point. Through tracking, I discovered that I allocated too much time to television and my phone. I reframed my excuse of not having enough time and focused instead on self-management, putting appointments on my calendar to exercise. You see, when I said there wasn't enough time, I was taking the focus and accountability off myself and putting it on something else, time. External blame replaced internal self-management. No wonder I was having difficulty succeeding; I believed it was not my fault! But in reality, this was not true. By managing myself I could attend to my goals each and every day. You may find it helpful to track the allocation of your time for a few weeks to see where your time is spent.

I am not so naïve to think that this is easy. Many of us are juggling several balls in the air hoping none crash to the ground. We are working parents and students, feel stuck in dead-end jobs, living paycheck to paycheck, floundering, and may even have a sense of being lost or living without purpose. I often hear that people are worried about their future. I share some of the same concerns as you. I don't have a magic wand to change things, but I can share what life taught me.

I've learned that the only thing I can change is myself. I cannot change others no matter how hard I try. I can change my situation, how I react to situations, and my expectations. If I am not happy about something in my little corner of the world, my choice is to complain or to change. I find that complaining doesn't usually work and just adds to my frustration. So, this leads us back to changing ourselves. In order to change ourselves we need to get kindergarten basic and look within.

Please allow me to share the process that worked for me. First, be honest with yourself. If you had a magic want, what would your ideal life look like? Write it down, every little detail. Don't forget to include your why. Next, write about your current situation. This will help you see the gap between what is and what you desire. This is the problem area from which we will develop goals. Create a list of things you can do to move closer to your ideal. Review the list and identify the most attainable and easiest thing you can do. Write this item in SMART goal format and implement. Be sure to include how you will track progress towards this goal.

My ideal was to have a healthy lifestyle, but there were many obstacles in my way. My problem area list was bit extensive, but I focused in on two: being overweight and a part-time job that interfered with my work-life balance. I realized that changes in my financial spending could afford me the opportunity to quit my part-time job. Through financial self-management, leaving my job was the most attainable goal. The SMART goal created in March stated that I would leave my part-time position by the end of August. It was specific, measurable, attainable, relevant and within a timeframe. Upon quitting, my lifestyle was immediately enhanced, one step closer to my ideal. But I was not there yet. I returned to my list of problem areas and identified the next attainable goal, weight loss, and began the process for success again.

It is said that insanity is doing the same thing over and over again and expecting a different result. That was me – the gerbil on the wheel, chasing the ideal, but getting nowhere fast. Changing my process, understanding ideals, identifying problem areas and creating attainable SMART goals is my current approach. While it appears cyclic, it is not. It is a focused approach addressing one goal at a time, continually closing the gap between what is and my desired ideal. It has worked for me and I believe it can work for you too!

About Gail A. Grenzig, PhD

For as long as she can remember, life-long learning has been the driving force behind all that Gail Grenzig does. This theme intersects her diverse endeavors as an author, public speaker, educator, licensed therapist, coach, and entrepreneur. Through a bit of education, guidance, support and empowerment, she believes each of us can achieve personal and professional fulfillment and success.

Gail believes in the power of connection. She discovered this first, as a teacher for students with disabilities, and later as a high school coach. Students wanted to belong, find direction, and most importantly, to believe in their own value and worth. It took time and work, but helping those students connect with others and more importantly, with themselves, was an invaluable life lesson and a driving force for her continued education, earning advanced degrees in administration, leadership, and a PhD in Counseling, Supervision, and Leadership. She has vast experience within the public-school settings as a teacher, assistant principal, director of pupil personnel, culminating as an assistant superintendent for human resources. She also owned Connections Counseling Center for many years. She served as an adjunct professor for several graduate counseling programs and is still working for Seton Hall University today. She presented at several national and local conferences within the counseling profession.

Throughout her life, Gail has a finger in many pies. At age 11, she took over her brother's paper route and hasn't stopped since. Goal-setting and personal accomplishments give her a sense of purpose. Lately, this took the form of entrepreneurship through real estate investing. She attended conferences, read books, watched podcasts, and networked with like-minded individuals. Within a short period of time, she formed a company and not only invested, but began to run local informative network meetings, coached others, and began to blog and speak at regional workshops and seminars about her experiences.

Gail knows the power of sharing experiences and telling a story. People want to connect and learn from others, but they don't always know how. When they see someone who is successful, they want to know how they did it. Why? Because we all want to live a self-directed life of purpose, one of which we can be proud. Gail recognizes this and is focused on writing and speaking about her experiences. As the founder of Authentic Connection Experts, she wants to help others create and direct their personal narrative leading to a life rich with meaning, purpose, and success. She believes that each of us has unique skills, talents, and beliefs within us. With guidance, support, and education, she believes that we can connect the dots, visualize and create our own purposeful life.

Gail A. Grenzig, PhD can be reached on:

- www.authenticconnectionexperts.com

Or, view her on Facebook at:

- Authentic Connection Experts

CHAPTER 23

UNVEILING THE TAPESTRY OF TRUE SUCCESS

BY GWEN MEDVED

Growing up amidst the wild expanses of Alaska, my earliest memories are interwoven with lessons from my father and the hum of society. The towering mountains and sweeping landscapes were my playground, where my imagination roamed freely, untethered by the constraints of the world beyond. In those formative years, I embraced a belief that would shape the trajectory of my life—the belief that happiness was woven into the fabric of love, support, and nurturing that thrived within the embrace of a white-picketed home.

My dreams, much like the pristine snow-covered wilderness of my home, were pure and innocent. I envisioned a life where I would find love, raise a family, and create a sanctuary of stability and security. My goals, my aspirations, and my definition of a successful life coalesced behind the imagery of a white picket fence—a symbol of the idyllic existence I longed to create. In the tapestry of my imagination, this dream was woven with threads of happiness, woven so intricately that the two seemed inseparable.

Yet, even as I clung to this vision with unwavering determination, the seeds of doubt were already planted within the fertile soil of my heart. The cracks in my foundation, however small, began to reveal themselves, hinting at the vulnerability that lay beneath the surface. Unbeknownst to me, my innocent dream was being shaped not only by the ideals I held but also by the tangled threads of my past.

Growing up in a home marked by dysfunction and discord, my yearning for familial perfection became more than just a dream—it became a lifeline. At the age of seventeen, I escaped the confines of my childhood home, carrying with me the weight of a promise unfulfilled. As I stepped into adulthood, I was determined to mold my life according to my own aspirations, to break free from the chains of my past, and to construct a reality that mirrored the pristine image I held dear.

With unwavering resolve, I embarked on a journey to create the life I had envisioned—a life defined by a successful marriage, adoring children, and deep ties within a nurturing community. Each achievement was a thread carefully woven into the intricate design of my white picket fence dream. From the outside, my life seemed flawless, a portrait of fulfillment and success. Yet, the ever-present undercurrent of anxiety and disquiet whispered of a deeper truth—a truth I was unwilling to confront.

The illusion I had so carefully crafted was shattered one fateful day, a cataclysmic moment of discovery that sent shockwaves through the foundation of my existence. The walls that had held my dream in place came crashing down, leaving me exposed and vulnerable. In the aftermath of the wreckage, I found myself grappling with the profound revelation that the life I had built was not built on a solid foundation of truth, but rather on the shifting sands of compromise, denial, and untruths.

The path to rediscovery was neither linear nor simple. It demanded a willingness to unlearn deeply ingrained patterns, to confront the origins of my self-imposed limitations, and to redefine success on my own terms. The journey within required me to dismantle the façade I had erected, to peel away the layers of pretense, and to confront the darkness that had lain dormant beneath the surface.

In the midst of this tumultuous journey, I made a radical decision—I chose to cast myself as both the problem and the solution. I delved into the depths of my roles as a wife, a mother, a daughter, a sister, a friend, and a member of my community. I recognized that the path to success lay not in external validation or the pursuit of an elusive white picket fence, but in the transformation of my own self. I resolved to become a better version of myself, to give more, be more, and do more, not for the sake of an illusory dream, but for the sake of my own growth and evolution.

Yet, this journey was not without its challenges. The terrain was treacherous, and the path was often obscured by the shadows of doubt and uncertainty. It required a willingness to let go of the safety net of a false reality and to confront the terrifying unknown that lay ahead. As I confronted the fractures in my foundation, I grappled with the painful truth—I had become a passenger in my own story, a secondary character in a narrative I had allowed others to dictate.

The weight of this realization was both liberating and agonizing. It demanded that I acknowledge the ways in which I had betrayed myself, and it compelled me to dismantle the illusory construct that had held me captive for so long. With every tear shed and every shard of falsehood shattered, I committed to a process of healing—a healing that required me to disentangle myself from the web of lies and to rediscover the essence of who I truly was.

As I embarked on this journey of self-love and transformation, I found myself surrounded by a supportive network of friends and family who became pillars of strength and guidance. Their unwavering presence provided the foundation upon which I could rebuild my sense of self and reclaim my authenticity. With their support, I began to unearth the power within me—the power to redefine success, to chart a new course, and to create a life aligned with my innermost truths.

In the crucible of self-discovery, I shed the toxic ties that had bound me and banished the negative self-talk that had perpetuated my self-imposed limitations. The relentless commitment to this process gradually stripped away the layers of victimhood and learned helplessness that had once defined me. I emerged from the cocoon of my former existence, reborn and empowered—a phoenix rising from the ashes of my shattered dream.

Amidst the rubble of my past, I discovered a newfound freedom—a freedom rooted in the alignment of my external life with my internal compass. Each step forward became a testament to my resilience, a declaration of my autonomy, and a tribute to the power of self-love. Through the process of shedding the layers of falsehood, I found myself drawn to the simple joys of life—the daily moments of joy that had once been overshadowed by the pursuit of an unattainable ideal.

As I walked the path of self-reclamation, I encountered moments of profound clarity, each milestone a testament to the strength and resilience that resided within me. I celebrated these victories, no matter how small, for they were tangible reminders of the progress I had made. Each step forward, no matter how tentative, propelled me further along the journey of redefining success on my own terms.

Embracing the lessons of my past and the wisdom gained from my journey, I emerged as a champion of authenticity—a beacon of light for those who, like me, yearned to break free from the shackles of societal expectations. With a newfound clarity of purpose, I embarked on a mission to connect with kindred spirits—individuals and brands committed to creating positive change in the world.

My vision extended beyond the confines of personal transformation; it encompassed a greater purpose—a purpose driven by a desire to inspire, facilitate, and connect. I became a bridge for those transitioning from the confines of an outdated definition of success to the boundless expanse of their own unique purpose. Together, we embarked on a journey of self-discovery, redefining success not as a destination, but as an ever-evolving process of growth and alignment.

In the wake of my transformation, I found myself no longer a bystander in my own narrative. Instead, I had become the author of my story, the architect of my destiny, and the curator of my own success. The tapestry of my life, once dominated by the illusion of a white picket fence dream, was now woven with the vibrant threads of authenticity, purpose, and self-love.

As I continue on this journey, I am guided by the unwavering belief that true success emanates from the alignment of one's heart, mind, and soul. Each day is a canvas, and I am the artist, painting the strokes of my life with intention and purpose. I have come to understand that the pursuit of success is not a linear path, but a lifelong odyssey—a constant process of redefinition, growth, and evolution.

In embracing this truth, I have discovered that the journey its
the destination—an intricate dance of self-discovery, self-acceptan
and self-expression. I no longer cling to the illusion of a static wh
picket fence, for I have transcended the limitations of that drear
Instead, I stand at the precipice of possibility, my heart open, my spir
unburdened, and my gaze fixed on the horizon of authentic success—
success that is uniquely mine, crafted with intention, and illuminated
by the radiant light of self-love.

As the tapestry of my life continues to unfold, I am reminded of the
profound power that comes from embracing one's true self. It is a
power that transcends societal norms, defies external expectations,
and propels us toward a life of purpose and fulfillment. My journey
from the confines of a false reality to the liberation of authenticity
has been a testament to the boundless potential that emerges when we
dare to redefine success on our own terms. Each day, I am grateful for
the lessons learned, the love discovered within, and the happiness that
flows from living a life rooted in truth, purpose, and the unwavering
embrace of one's own authentic self.

Embracing a lifelong journey of constantly redefining what success in
my life looks like and feels like has shown me that life rewards those
brave enough to redefine and take action, evolve, and grow each step
of the journey. It is an ongoing process, just like breathing is a constant
taking in of the new and releasing and exhaling the old. This way of
looking at life honors my authenticity and birth-given right to love and
happiness each day. I have come to realize that true success starts with
being true to myself and resisting the temptation to play a supporting
role in someone else's story.

Here are guiding questions and tools that have helped me in tuning
in to what guides me from within, and helps me curate and rule out
what comes from outside sources that distract me or block me from the
guidance of my own inner compass. These are exercises that can help
you gain clarity and identify your own key elements in redefining and
living what success means to you:

1. Reflect on your values and desires: Take the time to understand what
   truly matters to you and what brings you joy. Reflect on your core
   values and the things that make your heart sing. This self-reflection

' towards a definition of success that aligns with your

.elf-love and self-acceptance: Recognize that you are
.y of love, happiness, and success just as you are. Embrace self-
.ove and self-acceptance as the foundation for your journey. When
you believe in your own worth, you will attract relationships and
opportunities that support your authentic path.

3. Surround yourself with authentic relationships: Seek out genuine connections with people who embrace and support your true essence. Surround yourself with individuals who uplift and inspire you to be your best self. These relationships will provide you with the strength and encouragement to follow your own path.

4. Learn to say no: Practice setting boundaries and saying no to things that no longer serve you. Create space for joy and fulfillment by releasing toxic relationships, negative self-talk, and self-imposed limitations. Saying no is a powerful act of self-care and allows you to prioritize what truly matters to you.

5. Celebrate every milestone: Recognize and celebrate each milestone along your journey, no matter how small. Acknowledge your achievements and the progress you have made. This will fuel your motivation and remind you of the continuous growth and success you are experiencing.

6. Find a balance between self-love and serving others: Understand that success is not about sacrificing your own dreams for others, but about finding a balance between self-love and serving others. Discover ways to make a positive impact in the lives of those around you while staying true to your authentic self.

7. Embrace the journey: Remember that success is not a destination, but an ongoing process. Embrace the journey itself and find joy in the exploration and growth that it brings.

Accept that redefining success is a personal and unique experience and allow yourself to evolve and adapt along the way.

About Gwen

A Telly Award-Winning Producer, Gwen Medved is a successi. entrepreneur, author, and speaker with a deep commitment to family. Gwen works with individuals and companies here to make a difference for good. Gwen speaks with a 'compassion of truth, making her relatable and creating instant connection with clients and audiences telling her own unique and inspiring story what it takes to succeed and redefine what success means when opportunity is not handed to you.

Gwen leads in her field helping clients redefine success by creating alignment between their own individual integrity and authenticity with their brand identity, and business. Gwen has co-authored two Best-Selling books (including the Best-Seller, *Pillars of Success*, with Jack Canfield). Gwen works with women internationally to strategize brand clarity, navigating personal and professional blocks to develop and craft a life and business that aligns with their own authenticity, mission and purpose.

Gwen is founder & CEO of the Success School for Women, where she collaborates with other thought leaders, and mentors a portfolio of companies motivated by purpose and desire to create legacy impact. Gwen is an award-winning producer, bestselling author, and award-winning speaker and advocate for women and children.

Gwen has been seen in *Forbes, USA Today, Women's Health, Entrepreneur Magazine*, and has appeared on ABC, NBC, CBS and FOX television affiliates across the country, as well as YAHOO! News, CNBC, and MSNBC coast-to-coast.

Gwen is a member of The National Academy of Best-Selling Authors. She is a recipient of the EXPY award and the Quilly award. Gwen is a Telly Award-winning executive Producer of the DNA film, *It's Happening Right Here*, a film made to create prevention and spread awareness about child sex trafficking in the U.S.

Gwen holds a B.A. from Purdue University and an M.Ed. in Counseling and Human Services from DePaul University. She is a certified Canfield Transformational Trainer, Values-Based Leadership Coach and Health Coach, and advocate for women, children and families.

Gwen enjoys travelling and spending time with family and friends in the Midwest and Santa Monica, California. Future goals include lake house living with backyard chickens.

`com
.ɔolforwomen